SAVING INNOVATION

How to Harness the Incredible Promise of Innovation

SAVING INNOVATION

How to Harness the Incredible Promise of Innovation

....

MICHAEL DUGAN
with Chadd Scott

Mill City Press

Mill City Press, Inc.
212 3rd Avenue North, Suite 290
Minneapolis, MN 55401
612.455.2294
www.millcitypublishing.com

ISBN-13: 978-1-936780-89-1
LCCN: 2011937091

Book Design by Madge Duffy

Printed in the United States of America

PART I

**"Innovation – I like it,
but I'll never use it."**

PREFACE
Ft. Collins, Colorado

I never expected a 30-second conversation in Fort Collins, Colorado to change my life, but that's exactly what happened. I'm also hoping it revitalizes one of the most important business concepts of our era.

I'd been in the corporate world for almost 10 years focusing all of my attention on designing, developing and delivering innovation tools and techniques. I attended as many courses and seminars as possible, read every book on the subject and rapidly became known within the company I was working for as an expert on innovation. This company, Cargill Incorporated, is one of the world's largest privately held companies with business activities spanning every aspect of the food chain, in addition to financial services and risk management. It encompasses 130,000 employees in 1100 locations in 67 countries. Cargill leadership recognized early the potential benefits of innovation training and I was proud to be on the ground floor implementing the tools company-wide.

As a part of that mission, I had been invited to teach a two-day innovation tools seminar in Ft. Collins. Considering that my previous month's travel featured stops in Paris, Geneva and

Amsterdam, 48-hours in February chilled to 25 degrees wasn't my idea of a Rocky Mountain high. My first thought was, "What, all the conference space in Laramie was booked?"

After teaching a string of dynamic sessions and receiving the praise and adulation of my coworkers and course participants, I was on top of the world looking for a ladder to climb even higher. Had I heeded my father's expression, "the higher up the flag pole you get, the more your butt shows", I might have been in a more humble place to prepare myself for the professional haymaker I was about to receive in the middle of winter, in the middle of Colorado.

Fighting my rental Dodge Neon through a 50-mile-per hour crosswind from Denver to Ft. Collins, I resolved to ditch my snobby attitude and have the "rootinest, shootinest" innovation class this side of the Rio Grande. And I did.

The seminar went exactly as every other one I had taught recently: great energy, jokes, fun, ideas were generated and everyone enjoyed getting to know each other. For as much as I like to kid about the peculiarities and colloquialisms of every location I visit, I found my Ft. Collins group full of the same sort of bright professionals I'd come across in every other part of the world. They were scientists, plant managers and business leaders with a keen knowledge of their products and processes. No one was wearing chaps and everyone laughed politely at my "Pony Express" crack without taking offense. As had become routine, the session ended with enthusiastic applause and a line of people wanting to thank me for an incredible experience with offers to return soon to assist on other projects. Then came Doug. He was the last of the participants lined up to kiss the ring.

By this time I was usually out of business cards and had

exhausted my reservoir of compliments to hand back. I was ready to reach deep with this last fan. I wasn't prepared for how deeply I would need to reach.

Doug, a floor supervisor at a beef processing facility, came up to me with a huge smile on his face like the others. He enthusiastically mentioned how he enjoyed the seminar and "had a lot of fun, but to be honest with you Mike, I'll never use this."

I felt like the earth's core was sucking me toward it. Not only had I never heard negative feedback after one of my seminars, I'd never heard anything less than glowing praise.

Doug delivered a knockout punch to my chin I never saw coming. I wobbled. I was stunned. Stunned silent. I literally couldn't say a word. I'm sure it was only a second or two, but if felt like minutes went by before I responded. I wanted to fire back instantly with something inspiring or clever, but I couldn't.

My classes were dynamic, interactive, educational, empowering; how could Doug not want to incorporate my teachings from the past two days into his business? He was bright, he'd been an engaged participant; he laughed along with everyone else. Doug could see the value of innovation and understood the concepts I had presented. When I finally regained my senses, I asked him, "why not?"

He said the only things he was measured on at his facility were production numbers and safety index.

I had no response.

I'm embarrassed to say that my first thought was, "That's your problem. I can't force you to use these tools. If you see the value of innovation and think it can help, yet you consciously choose not to use it, shame on you and good luck getting the results you have always gotten until you get squeezed out by your competition."

I wanted to put the problem on him, but this immediately didn't feel right.

I paused and restarted the conversation. After several minutes I came to better understand his location's culture and realized how similar his story was to others I had heard. His business was filled top to bottom with a "get it done" attitude; his facility's goals were to generate quickly and safely as much product as possible, a goal for which the facility was perfectly designed to achieve.

To expect Doug's team to modify the way it had been operating and thinking about challenges for the past 25 years in a two-day session was ridiculous. We both agreed there was no way for any business to shift from being production focused to innovation focused simply by teaching some fun tools. It was going to take a wholly different approach. I sincerely thanked Doug for his feedback and made a commitment to think about how to make real changes in my approach to innovation.

Within 15 minutes of wrapping up my conversation with Doug, I was back in the Neon with the front range of the Rocky Mountains on my right and the Great Plains stretching endlessly on my left. The clear blue sky couldn't have been in starker contrast to the storm clouds roiling in my mind. I had 70 minutes driving south on I-25 to let that criticism permeate my brain.

I should have said this.

I should have said that.

What did I not do; what did I not get across?

At each exit – U.S. Highway 34, State Hwy. 66, County Road 119, (traveler's note, there aren't many cities in Colorado) – I wanted to turn around, sit down with Doug, dig through his head and figure out where my approach went astray. I needed to connect with him, better understand his employees and problems. I had a compulsion to understand how I could fix this crisis right now, but all I could do was drive.

Every positive remark I had ever gotten was left in Ft. Collins as Doug's comment had headline billing in my thoughts.

I started questioning everything.

I wondered how many of the thousands of other participants I had taught felt the same way, but were too timid to speak up.

As I thought about my classes it occurred to me that all of the positive comments were directed towards how engaging a teacher I was, how entertaining the class was, how high my energy was, how fun the tools were. My feedback wasn't about how excited participants were to use the tools I presented or how the seminar had been so helpful. My follow-up notes didn't talk about progress made as a result of what I had taught.

It was wonderful being liked and being thought of as entertaining and funny, but was anyone using this? Shouldn't I be hearing success stories like how the implementation of tools generated new ideas, made the company more money, cut waste, did something?

Then it hit me like that anvil that drops on Wile E. Coyote stopping him dead in his tracks. Doug had exposed a critical weakness with how I was teaching and thinking about innovation. Somewhere between Buffalo Bill's Grave and Museum and the Sandstone Ranch it became clear to me that application, not philosophy, needed to be the focal point. If my participants were unwilling or unable to put what I had presented into action, what was the use?

With the lights of Denver coming into view on the horizon, I had to put my mind back in the moment. The Neon needed refueling, I faced a slog through the notoriously long Denver airport security line and if I couldn't comfort my thoughts, I sure could comfort my stomach with some quesadillas and an ice-cold Fat Tire Amber Ale from New Belgium Brewing – Ft. Collins' foremost contribution to Western Civilization.

I started to let Doug go. With the idea of sleeping in my own bed becoming more and more of a reality following each mile I ticked off, I began to hope Doug's comment was his isolated thought. I tried convincing myself that I shouldn't change everything I've done and believed about teaching innovation because of one person.

I had worked with and been taught by the globally recognized leaders in the field. My methods mirrored the cutting edge of innovation training taking place in the most successful companies in the world. I even had my alibi ready to go: I was too busy moving from location to location giving seminars to worry about extensive follow-up.

I had 160,000 employees to reach in 60 different businesses in 60 countries; when was I going to have the time to think of how innovation tools could possibly apply to the uniqueness of each business? I didn't have time to create, develop and teach the subsequent training that would be necessary to make my tools applicable specifically to Doug's location – and Scott's and Jane's and Randy's and Melissa's.

My job was to distribute these tools and techniques to as many people as possible. Course participants needed to take on the responsibility of implementation. These were smart people. I had led them to the water and shown them how beneficial it was to drink. They needed to figure out how to customize the straw for their facility.

I gained enough comfort from this rationalization to fly home

without going crazy. I took the weekend off trying to push Doug
to the margins of my thoughts, but he kept creeping back.

The Morning After

In the office Monday morning my colleagues asked me about
the session. I told them it was fantastic and that I received the
most valuable piece of feedback.

I felt vulnerable as I retold the story of Doug's comment and
how my approach to training events had been missing the mark
for years. I explained how my focus had been misguidedly placed
on content and delivering a dynamic experience. I had ignored
application and helping users launch their innovation efforts. My
assumption was that participants would take on the responsibility
of making the application and figuring out where to start. Tools
and fun were my emphasis.

While reviewing my recent training requests, it occurred to
me that I had become a corporate entertainer. I received calls from
district managers, who had to fill a couple hours at their annual
meeting, and they wanted me to present some innovation points.
Another group gave me a standing invitation to their summer
meeting. Generating results through innovation was secondary to
them. I was just invited to attend these meetings because I always
put on a good show. I felt flattered to be wanted, but the long-
term innovation benefits were negligible. Innovation was something the company was talking about, so, "Let's call Michael!"
These groups and individuals didn't care about innovation tools.
What they were asking for was entertainment. People liked me
and I made them laugh. I was creative, motivating and entertaining, word got around, and without realizing it I had become my

company's combination of Carrot Top and Tony Robbins.

My approach towards innovation wasn't working. I wasn't sure what the solution was, but I knew there had to be a different and/or better approach. For innovation training to be effective, my entire philosophy towards its implementation had to change.

Change

What I experienced in Ft. Collins began a personal journey for me to develop what I hoped would become the most user-friendly innovation strategies and tools available.

In the coming months I started to open my mind to innovation. I took a wider view. If application had been overlooked, what else had the current thought neglected in favor of a tools-exclusive approach?

I started thinking about business cultures, goal setting and a total system of innovation. I examined how the philosophy of innovation was being distributed to all levels of the company; where was it succeeding, where was it not meeting expectations. I wondered which tools are most essential to learn and understand to create a foundation for innovation. I heard people's frustrations about not knowing exactly where to start this process.

I began to ask questions when my business contacts called requesting my services. I asked what innovation training they'd done previously. What tools are being used and how have they been integrated into daily operation? What is the business goal or result they want to accomplish through my training? What behaviors would they like to see their employees embracing as a result of this session? What in their structure, measurements or culture will support those new behaviors?

It took exactly one of these conversations to realize the person on the other end of the phone was not only unused to those types of questions, but had no idea how to respond to them. This confusion confirmed that though businesses sought innovation, they gave less thought to how training, goals, culture, people and results were linked. Training alone does not produce results; it was incorrectly believed one would follow the other.

The subject for which I had devoted my passion and staked my professional career on needed saving. With a futures mindset I could see the demise of innovation as a widespread business practice.

I needed to strip innovation down, take it out of the boardrooms and away from the jargon, tailor it to the people responsible for putting it place. I had to stop training innovation with an emphasis on laughs and start training innovation with an emphasis on results. I needed to start teaching with Doug in mind. Going forward, the participant had to come first.

In order for innovation to flourish I would need to spotlight my training on the following attributes:

- Creating an innovative culture
- Properly identifying goals
- Establishing the fundamentals of idea generation
- Supporting innovation through leadership

It all came down to culture, goals, tools and people.

When I mention "innovation capital of the world" what cities do you think of? Palo Alto, California? New York? Tokyo? Geneva? Not one person in six billion thinks of Ft. Collins, Colorado. Well, make that one person, me, and I think about it every day.

CHAPTER 1
Why Innovation Needs Saving

Cheese-stuffed-crust pizza. I love it. It's hard for me to remember a time before it existed. Then it was innovated and my life has never been the same.

Any change, advancement or progression that's ever taken place in business, like cheese stuffed-crust pizza, has been the result of innovation. Innovation gave us the wheel, the radio, the Clapper.

Without innovation there is no progress. Since the Dark ages every successive generation of people have enjoyed a quality of life superior to their predecessors. Our ability to innovate and continually deliver what had previously been thought of as impossible is responsible for this progress. More than merely boosting profit margins, innovation drives our quality of life from medical advancements to cheesier pizza.

When your car's global position system tells you exactly where to drive to get to the nearest Italian restaurant in a town you've never been to or you walk through an electronics store surrounded by increasingly smaller and more powerful cell phones, televisions, cameras and radios, innovation appears to be thriving. Daily advancements in technology, our ever-lengthening life expectancy, instantaneous global communication and a galaxy of consumer choices few ever imagined support a belief that innovation will continue to reliably answer our toughest questions.

That may be the case at Intel, NASA or the Johns Hopkins Hospital where billions are spent yearly developing the futuristic innovations we now take for granted, but what about your business? What about the innovation efforts for those of us without research budgets, government grants or teams of employees dedicated to "what's next?"

Here, innovation is in danger.

Innovation is in danger at schools, communities and government. It's in danger at small businesses, teams and at the individual level. The extraordinary power of innovation to overcome challenges and its life-changing potential is dying in the hands of the majority of people attempting to realize it.

I have found through my contacts, seminars and conventions that a handful of businesses are winning through innovation. These businesses are experiencing dynamic growth and record profits through a historically bad economic environment by valuing and practicing a process of innovation which has allowed them to continually operate faster, smarter and at the leading edge of their fields.

I have found that to be uncommon. Most businesses are not succeeding at their innovation efforts. Not only are they not succeeding, they are failing miserably. As a result, their desire to continue pursuing innovation is waning.

If a majority of businesses abandon their pursuit of innovation allowing it to become the sole property and responsibility of the Boeings and Exxon/Mobiles and Pfizers, its potential will have been annihilated. Giant corporations, mid-size businesses, small teams and individuals must fuel innovation equally for us to collectively and fully reap its astounding benefits.

There are only 500 "Fortune 500" companies. We expect these companies to innovate because they have extensive resources to devote to developmental projects and time and again their research has brought new products to market. Five hundred sounds like a big number, but it represents a tiny fraction of the total number of businesses in America and worldwide. These top 500 companies can't possibly be expected to do all of our innovating.

There are 1.8 million small businesses in New York State alone. Even without the same size budgets and workforces of the "Fortune 500" companies, no reason exists why they can't be equally as innovative, if not more innovative. One great advantage they have is their flexibility, nimbleness and ability to act quickly, all problems for multi-national corporations with boards of directors, shareholders, layers of management and chains of command. The Disney's and McDonald's of the world are doing a good job innovating, where the potential for exponential growth with innovation exists is with smaller companies who are trying to find their footing with innovation.

Innovation needs saving at the ground floor of business and industry and I intend to save it.

Most businesses rightly believe they have the people and ideas necessary to achieve their goals. The desire and resources to succeed through innovation exist; so do unseen impediments to its useful implementation. Before I could save innovation, I had to identify the poison pills wrecking a body that so badly wants to live.

When their character finally became clear to me I was shocked at how thoroughly the body had been infected.

The Barbaric Manager

I uncovered an employee working to kill innovation: the *"Barbaric Manager."* Squashing ideas that could become breakthroughs because of his own insecurity or ego he tops the list as innovation's enemy number one.

The barbarian uses the power of his position to crush employee ambition, ideas and engagement. A combination of ignorance and arrogance fuels this manager's desire to conquer and subjugate his staff. Both aggressive and weak, this prototypical bully stifles the creativity and imagination of his employees and makes sure innovation doesn't happen through the repetitive and dismissive, insulting, belittling, demolition of thoughts and ideas. Eventually his employees lose hope of making a difference and just stop trying.

The best innovation tools and strategies in the world go nowhere with this barbarian at the gate.

While there are classic managerial errors from history that everyone recognizes – Custer's Last Stand, the leaders who watched as General Motors went from the world's largest company to bankruptcy – far more commonplace are the millions of middle managers, branch managers, supervisors, and shift bosses who ruin innovation on a smaller level.

Senior leaders may drive strategic direction, but it's the infinite layers of sub-managers who ensure that direction takes hold – or doesn't. These managers have their boots on the ground every day at the store and facility level and wield enormous influence because they interact most regularly with employees – the vast untapped resource of ideas that every business possesses and few utilize.

To emphasize the importance that this stratum of management has over companies and employees, a Gallup Poll of 1,000,000 U.S. workers released in 2009 found that the number one reason people quit their jobs is a bad boss or immediate supervisor.

"People leave managers not companies...in the end, turnover is mostly a manager issue," Gallup wrote in its survey findings. It also determined that poorly managed work groups are on average 50 percent less productive and 44 percent less profitable than well-managed groups.

The *Barbaric Manager* has been widely parodied on TV and in movies and it's something that most of us, unfortunately, have personal experience with. One of the best examples of this character and his toxic influence on employees and companies comes from radio personality Howard Stern's biography, "Private Parts."

After drawing huge audiences in Detroit and then Washington, D.C., Stern was hired by WNBC radio in New York City. It was his dream job in his home town. Stern would find that his dream became a nightmare and the reason was largely because of a series of vicious, insecure and hostile *Barbaric Managers*.

Admittedly, Stern isn't the easiest employee to manage because of his wild antics and enormous ego, but those attributes are commonplace in the entertainment business and his talents and results are undeniable. At WNBC, Stern was verbally abused, insulted and humiliated by his *Barbaric Manager*.

A few of this individual's lowlights when it came to "managing" Stern were copying and distributing memos throughout the company which detailed his criticisms of Stern's work, even janitors received copies. This manager attempted to drive a wedge between Stern and the other members of his show by telling the supporting cast that the company had no money to pay them raises because "Howard has taken it all."

Instead of embracing Stern's talent and attempting to bring him more in line with the company's practices by appealing to their mutual interest of generating listeners and attracting sponsors, this *Barbaric Manager* continually tried to crush Stern's imagination, creativity, and passion for his job by making the work environment as uncomfortable, combative and needlessly petty as possible.

This manager would return to obscurity after leaving the station while Stern – after being fired by WNBC – would land a job with the competition, taking them to number-one in the ratings. His show would go on to become syndicated nationally, expanded to television, and serve as the foundation of a media dynasty, all the while making millions of dollars for the companies and managers that supported him.

The *Barbaric Manager* drives away top performers every day bankrupting his company of talented people. Left behind are employees who have no ambition or ideas and those showing up only for the paycheck. How many game-changing innovations have walked out the door because of a barbarian?

How can you tell the difference between an incompetent manager, a dope or someone simply in over his head and my *Barbaric Manager*? Stealing a routine from comic Jeff Foxworthy, "you might have a *Barbaric Manager* if ...

... it takes months to hear about something you did well, but minutes to hear about something you did wrong."

... lying, intimidation, cronyism and evasion are his go-to management tools"

... people stop talking when he enters a room."

... you love what you do, but have to talk yourself into

showing up every morning, and out of quitting every night."

... you can recall with amazing detail a degrading, humiliating, embarrassing, sickening, nauseating, or painful interaction you had with him"

... the last time you had a great idea your next thought was 'why bother?'"

... he's eager to hear your needs and eager to tell you how to get along without them"

... you've ever thought how easy it would have been to manage the Yankees under George Steinbrenner by comparison."

... at any moment you think he'll have the company invade Poland.

Consciously or unconsciously these managers are stifling innovation across all geographies and throughout companies large and small.

With one contaminant diagnosed, I continued my examination of the ailing body of innovation. I would quickly find a second virus draining its life. This virus does not come in the form of a person, but as a mindset.

Unrealistic expectations about what goals can be achieved through innovation training and how quickly they can be met are crippling its use.

The iPod of...

In the 1990's and 2000's, we all saw companies making billions of dollars thanks to incredibly innovative ideas. Businesses were enamored by the potential for astronomical economic returns from new products and services. The crown jewel of these was the iPod.

Seemingly overnight, Apple had unveiled a completely new product. A computer company revolutionized the music industry by innovating a device that seemed straight out of "The Jetsons." Ten years ago, Apple was not in the portable music business; today it owns more than 70-percent of the market. Others saw these results and wanted to duplicate them.

The iPod replaced the light bulb as the new symbol for innovation and everyone wanted to jump into the innovation pool so they could develop their own magnum opus. Businesses thought that by introducing an innovation tool at the monthly meeting or conducting a playful ideation session at the company picnic, revolutionary products would fall out of the sky and everyone would drive a Maserati.

A food business team I worked with rallied around the theme of wanting to create the "iPod of meat." Those were their exact words. They didn't intend to make a portable mp3 player out of beef; they wanted to innovate the next new idea in meat that would completely transform their industry the way the iPod did for portable music.

I believe audacious goals are admirable; however, a better goal for this group would have been to become the "Apple of meat." Instead of focusing solely on bringing a once-in-a-lifetime product to market, this team should have focused on becoming the most innovative company in its industry which would result in the regular development of once-in-a-lifetime products, such as Apple developed with the iPod, iPhone, iPad and others.

Businesses who tried innovation and didn't realize instantaneous market-shifting results felt duped and betrayed by the great promise of innovation. That wasn't innovation's fault. Innovation doesn't work that way. Nothing works that way.

This fervor reminded me of my own attempts at wanting to lose weight and become more physically fit. I saw pictures with sculpted models and wanted those same results. I thought, "I can do that."

No I couldn't.

I didn't have a nutritionist or a personal trainer. I wasn't willing to spend four or five hours every week working out hard. I wasn't willing to make the lifestyle changes necessary to achieve these goals like cutting out fast food, reducing my alcohol consumption and sacrificing free time for strenuous exercise.

I thought, "Maybe there is an easier way." There were plenty of quick fixes available: "The South Beach Diet," "The Green Tea Diet," "Thirty Minutes a Week to a Healthier You," The "Ab-Roller."

Nothing worked. I became discouraged by my lack of immediate progress and quit.

Businesses made the same choices with innovation that I, and millions of other dieters, make every day – and got the same results. Businesses lacked the commitment to a culture of innovation so they instituted quick and fun training sessions to see what ideas they could generate. Innovation training had turned into the Thighmaster – it's fun, its fast, you can do it while watching TV and you'll develop million dollar ideas in just 15 short minutes a week!

Wrong.

In a frenzied rush for instant results without effort and dedication, business quickly lost hope and gave up after their wildest fantasies about creating the next iPod weren't realized within weeks. Two days before your 20th high school reunion you won't be able to do 100 sit-ups and have six-pack abs and no business can create the next iPod following a single two-hour innovation training.

It took Apple one year to create the iPod. This doesn't sound like much until you realize Apple had approximately 30 full-time employees devoting all of their efforts and energies to nothing but its development. Also, Apple had a culture already in place that fully supported innovation, making results more likely to be achieved. Apple valued innovation, followed a highly developed process of innovation, and held firm to its belief that the process would deliver.

The companies that excel at innovating, like Apple, work on it regularly not expecting quick fixes the same as people who are in great shape work out regularly not expecting immediate results.

To innovative companies, innovation helps define them, it permeates their everyday operations, and they understand that results will come over time. These companies emphasize the importance of innovation and sacrifice other areas to fully support it in the same way that fit people make fitness a part of their everyday life. Fit people are fit because they leave the bar early to get to sleep so they can wake up at 5:30 AM and be at the gym. They take the extra 10 minutes each morning to pack a lunch so they don't eat fast food. It's not an accident that the people who are in great shape are in great shape or that innovative companies are innovative. Their results are owed to hard work, commitment, sacrifice and realistic expectations.

Had I focused on making gradual and consistent changes to the way I approached eating and exercise, I'd be incredibly pleased with how my body looked. Instead, I went from fad to fad, trying a series of quick fixes that had no chance of working to help me reach my goals.

Businesses, likewise, have been grasping at unproven, quick-fix gimmicks to help them develop the next profit-bulging product and have been experiencing weak results.

Had a company or team instead committed to a sound and sustained process of innovation instead of seeking out get-rich-quick devices, it would now be on its way to being thought of as the "Apple" of its industry. Like the millions of pieces of exercise equipment sitting unused in garages, innovation training manuals are gathering dust all over the world because they didn't deliver the foolishly optimistic immediate results that they promised and which were expected by users.

Due to innovation's inability to meet the absurd expectations heaped upon it, it's on the verge of being dumped by many companies who have given it a try – even though those efforts were often misguided.

Basics Are Beautiful

The third major roadblock to effective innovation comes from a *disregard for the basics.*

When people want to develop new ideas, they tend to think the more fantastic and complex the tools they use, the more fantastic and groundbreaking their ideas will be.

The opposite is true. In the same way that a strong foundation in the basics is essential to a professional athlete or musician, a strong foundation in the basics is essential to an effective innovator.

The simple and basic idea generation tools which have been used and proven effective for years still are today and always will be. Unfortunately, they have been passed over in favor of high-concept creativity tools and games which require years of experience and hours of training to perfect.

How can basic brainstorming be more effective in generating ideas than a proprietary "system" of idea generation backed up by a $500-an-hour instructor with an Ivy-League degree and a trunk full of visual aides, gadgets and toys? Complicated seldom beats simple and it certainly doesn't when it comes to innovating.

Innovation consultants are often guilty of this crime. With the best of intentions, these would-be innovation advocates are actually doing more harm than good by presenting innovation in a way most businesses and individuals are unable to use.

These consultants speak to a company's leadership, but the majority of employees can't translate their 10,000-foot view, boardroom jargon into action or results.

Instead of focusing on the basics, consultants jump to advanced tools and nuanced philosophy. Without any foundation in innovation established or a culture set up to support it, employees struggle to use these strategies effectively.

No business would introduce an advanced new computer system, laud its tremendous potential benefits to employees, then leave the boxes full of hardware and software on their desks for them to put together and figure out with no instruction manual. That very situation is often found in a company's innovation efforts. Frustration soon sets in and an inevitable dismissal of innovation occurs as the front-line employees charged with making it happen never get a handle on what to do or how exactly to use it.

I once attended a seminar where the speaker was promoting the use of a visual based activity to improve brainstorming. The technique involved the use of LEGOs. Teams were asked to define their business' problem, after which each team member was instructed to build with LEGOs a metaphorical model of how they viewed the problem, or who they'd like the problem to look like.

Upon construction, individuals were then required to present their models to the group, explaining what they had built and how the model could translate into ideas for solving the problem. Then brainstorming would begin.

Think of all the inherit skills this exercise demands to make it successful: transforming thoughts into three-dimensional models, building things with your hands, presentation and descriptive abilities, and understanding what metaphors are.

While this is great for team building and idea generation for advanced teams, this method and similarly advanced techniques are complex and inefficient for teams wanting to get started with the basics.

The *Barbaric Manager, unrealistic expectations* and a *disregard for the basics*, constitute the smoking, drinking and sedentary lifestyle to the body of innovation.

Innovation needs saving now because the business world has bought in to its promise. Companies both large and small recognize innovation as the best way to achieve their goals. The spotlight shines on innovation and it must deliver or be shuffled to the back of the deck.

While innovation lies in critical condition, its spirit lives. That's the good news.

If you're already trying to innovate and not getting the results you want, don't give up; if you've yet to attempt innovation, you're not too late.

There are steps you can take to resuscitate innovation. The

tools, techniques and approaches in the following chapters will give you a foundation for true innovation that will be practical, applicable and easily understood regardless of your industry, experience or perceived lack of creativity.

CHAPTER 2
The Language of Innovation

When I was growing up, my dad drove an 18-wheeler. At home, he parked it in the community college parking lot at the end of the street because our driveway was too small. One morning he asked me to fetch something out of the cab. When I got to the truck, the driver's side window was broken, the door was open, and the inside had been ransacked.

I called my dad and he told me to stay by the truck and dial 9-1-1. I called the cops and told the dispatcher that I had been robbed.

In a frantic voice, the woman at the other end of the line said, "Are you ok? Are you hurt? Are you still in danger?"

I was confused by the panic and urgency in her voice.

I said "No, my dad's truck was broken into and I'm just calling you to make a police report." The woman sighed, "Oh, you mean you were burgled, not robbed."

Like most people, I used the words "robbed" and "burgled" interchangeably, but in fact, while similar, some distinct and important differences in the words' meanings do exist. A robbery involves taking something from someone, in their presence, by violence or threat. Burglary is breaking in and taking something without violence.

For police to respond to these crimes and handle them appropriately, they have to know exactly what you mean. Police officers and dispatchers must understand the subtlety and nuance of these terms to avoid confusion and an improper prioritization of resources. If the police used "burglary" and "robbery" interchangeably the way most of us do, think of the mistakes that would be made, possibly life threatening mistakes. Cops would be responding to burglaries that had happened hours ago before attending to robberies where the suspects may still be in the vicinity of the crime and the victim in danger. To law enforcement, a robbery and a burglary are different crimes, to most of us, all we know is that our stuff is gone.

Every profession has its own language, subtle differences in word usage that must be clearly defined and understood by those working daily in the field in order to communicate effectively.

Innovation is no different. If you are going to be a skilled innovator you need to know these terms and what their precise definitions are.

The first and most misunderstood word in the field of innovation is "innovation" itself. There is an assumption that everyone knows what "innovation" means; I believe the reverse is true.

Because the word "innovation" is used so casually, I'm guessing most people aren't exactly sure what it means and what it doesn't. It's a common enough word, we've all used it, but ask someone to define it and you'll get as many answers as people you ask. We know innovation has something to do with the generation of new ideas, beyond that, its definition seems individual to the user.

For innovation to be successful, we have to know what it means – specifically. Added to the uncertainty surrounding "innovation" are these commonly used and misused terms: "creativity," "imagination," and "invention." Having an unclear understanding of the vocabulary of innovation creates confusion which adds to the reasons for its potential demise. For innovation to deliver on its promise, we all need to be speaking the same language.

IMAGINATION: The unbounded vision in ones mind. It's the power to dream and visualize scenarios that are not based in reality or constrained by our work structures and business mindset limitations. Imagination is free and without risk.

Imagination takes place in the mind and our mind never shuts off. If you are trying to remember a person's name or the name of a song you heard on the radio, when do you remember it? For most of us it is in shower, right before we go to bed, or in the middle of the night. Why? Because our brain never shuts off.

Our brain's imagination is a tremendous untapped resource. It works 24 hours a day every day of the year. We need to learn to tap into this power and mine it effectively.

Mining our imagination leads to creativity.

CREATIVITY: Taking the visions of imagination and putting them into ideas. The root of creativity is "create." Creating something tangible from imagination. An idea has to get out of someone's head and be communicated effectively before it can become anything. These ideas can then be managed, evaluated and acted upon.

People are already imagining - we need to help them become creative. When a business establishes a creative environment, people will begin to share the visions in their minds.

When I talk to groups about "imagination" and "creativity," I always ask participants to share stories of ideas they had for new products, products they would see on store shelves years later frustrated that someone else had made millions of dollars off them. I've heard people talk about having the idea for MTV, eBay, and rollerblades long before they came into existence.

These stories are told with an equal sense of pride for the idea and irritation at the lost opportunity of having done nothing with it. I've experienced this myself with my idea for the self-waving flag. Through the years I repeatedly saw flags lay limp at sporting events during the triumphant moment of the playing of the national anthem. I told myself I should invent a flagpole with an air pump at the base and holes at the top that could blow wind waving the flag dramatically on cue.

During the opening ceremonies at the 2008 Beijing Olympic Games, the world saw my self-waving flag. But it wasn't my invention. It had only been my idea, my imagination and creativity; I thought of it, but that's where I left it.

I've heard hundreds of these stories which prove the ideas are out there. Ideas are important to the process of innovation and equally important is taking those ideas and doing something with them. Taking action on those ideas leads to invention.

INVENTION: Taking the ideas generated through creativity and producing a tangible, well-constructed prototype or concept of a product, service or improved work process. An idea developed sufficiently in concept or form to be testable.

Car companies are great at inventing, constantly imagining new cars and features. They create these products by making sketches and models, eventually producing prototypes to acquire market feedback.

Most of those cars or features never see a showroom; the concept is scrapped, shelved for a later date, or recycled for further refinement. However, if a prototype receives strong feedback and research shows there exists a market for it, the prototype can become mass-produced and delivered to consumers becoming an innovative product.

Once a prototype sells in the marketplace, it has become an innovation.

INNOVATION: Innovation marks the point at which people pay you for the products and services you've developed. Innovation is the end result – when a value from imagination, creativity and invention has been realized.

Companies don't engage in the process of innovation merely to have fun or increase employee engagement, they do it to make or save money. Innovation is the point where cost savings have been realized or customers purchase new products or services. Until results have been experienced, innovation has not taken place.

Most people confuse creativity with innovation. Simply generating ideas does not mean you're innovating. You haven't innovated until you've experienced a reward for all the work done in the previous steps. Innovation is not an exercise, it is results.

There is a *process* to innovating which includes imagination, creativity and invention, however, when you read the word "innovation" in this book, it refers to a product, service or process improvement which has generated results. I will further explain the *process* of innovation which features the stages previously referenced and can also include marketing, sales, research, accounting, management and a number of other steps. As innovators, we must comprehend that simply undertaking this process does not equal "innovation," innovation occurs when results are experienced.

The Process of Innovation

We take imagination, translate it into ideas, create a prototype, and then implement to receive value.

Think of these terms along a time line. Let's use entrepreneur Richard Branson's Virgin Galactic as an example.

Branson was a child when man first landed on the moon and it was an achievement that inspired him deeply. He considers it a pivotal moment in his life. Space travel became something he wanted to experience and with a man on the moon in 1969 it seemed reasonable to assume that at some point in the future, as technology advanced, he'd be able to have that experience. This is the *imagination* phase: Richard Branson with a vision for ordinary people being able to experience space travel.

Branson would go on to build a business empire, but nothing seemed to be happening with that whole "space travel for the rest of us" dream.

In 1991, fed up with a lack of progress and still inspired by his desire to go to space, Branson developed the idea of Virgin Galactic. Virgin Galactic would be a private company offering space travel for everyday citizens. This is the *creativity* phase. Branson's imagination wanted space travel for everyone. With no one stepping forward to make it happen, he decided to. His idea of commercialized space travel, put on paper, given a name, made tangible, made available for others to assess was creative.

This is not yet innovation. Branson had a dream, a vision, an idea, a possibility and that's all it was. Now he needed to figure out how to make it happen.

Imagination leads to creativity which leads to *invention* and this is where Branson went next. Branson traveled the world seeking out the insight of innumerable physicists, pilots, astronauts and engineers picking their brains about the viability of the project. He eventually met an engineer with whom he developed an immediate connection and this man, Burt Rutan, developed prototypes for what Branson's Virgin Galactic spaceship might look like. Virgin Galactic began to invent model spaceships, a process that continues to this day.

While Branson's scientists and engineers continued to work on the invention phase, Branson put another team together working on the *innovation* stage where he looked to monetize the project.

Branson, in addition to his marketers and salespeople, began taking Virgin Galactic, and the possibility of space travel, to the public. Virgin Galactic aimed for a 2010 launch at a cost of $200,000 per person. At the time of this writing, late 2010, Virgin Galactic has 300 fully paid travelers, with a waiting list, and more than $40 million in deposits.

That's the power of innovation! An idea, coming from anywhere and inspired by anything, made tangible, followed through and developed into reality. The result is a new product, service or efficiency improvement.

Innovation is a process in which imagination, creativity and invention are all important, separate, and clearly defined phases.

Now that you know what those terms mean and how they apply to innovation, there's an important question that must be answered.

PART II

The Chicken or the Egg

CHAPTER 3
Which Comes First: Culture or Tools?

So now what?

Once a commitment to innovation has been made the natural inclination becomes grabbing for tools and holding brainstorming sessions and meetings to generate ideas.

That seems reasonable enough. Tools generate ideas, they are tangible and can be put on paper and taught. Progress toward the next big breakthrough in your business could seemingly be made this afternoon.

Every team I've worked with finds itself exactly where you are now and thinks, "We get it! Let's get to the fun stuff! Let's get the ideas rolling!"

While tools are necessary, without a supportive culture in place to properly utilize them, they're virtually useless. Take Doug from Ft. Collins, the tools I presented him were first rate, but since his facility's culture didn't support innovation, he had no way of putting them into effectual practice.

Culture Eats Tools for Breakfast

Stop by your local gym on the way home from work tonight.

Pop your head in the door and look at all that great equipment, all those great fitness tools – barbells, dumbbells, strength machines, cardio machines, steppers, bikes, balls, rowers. With access to all those great tools, how come there are still so many out of shape people at that gym, and every other one as well? I promise you it's not because they just signed up.

For starters, most members don't have the first idea about how to properly use those tools, but the lack of a commitment to fitness from a complete time, effort and lifestyle standpoint proves to be the primary reason. They haven't created within their own lives a culture that fully supports being in shape. The best gym equipment in the world will not get someone in shape if they continue to smoke, drink soda, eat greasy sausage pizza before going to bed and only use that equipment 10 minutes a week.

Conversely, to a person truly committed to fitness, tools are almost unnecessary to achieve that end. Running, body weight exercises, swimming, jumping rope, eating a balanced diet – those things require only rudimentary tools and if they're worked at hard and consistently will lead to fitness 100% of the time.

If being in shape was simply a matter of having the right tools, every gym member would look fantastic. The same situation exists with innovation.

If successful innovation were only about having the best tools, every business using creativity tools would be experiencing results because most of the tools in use are effective. When the use of these tools fails to generate results you'll most often find an unsupportive culture as the reason why.

A business committing to innovation and using a tools-first approach without having a culture that supports their use will never realize the results it expects. Frustration will set in, same as with all those gym members who wander aimlessly from machine to machine with no results, and the effort will be given up.

My years of experience have shown me conclusively the establishment of an innovative culture must come before the introduction of tools because that culture will deliver more consistent and better results than the tools alone.

Culture works. A culture of innovation is sustainable and long term. Culture delivers results around the clock, within and outside of the office. Culture overcomes problems and challenges for both the present and the future and it engages everyone.

Tools are limited. Tools help you in a moment. Tools solve only the problems they are specifically asked to help solve within the limited time frame they are being used and by the relatively few people allowed to use them. Plus, tools work only if the culture exists which allow them to work.

When a team places its primary innovation focus on tools, innovation all too often becomes about the tools. Innovation needs to be about the results. Time and again I have seen tool-focused groups become enamored with a cool, new, fun creativity game or activity and then ask me, "Can you come and facilitate a session where we can try that new tool?" The problem to be solved has become secondary to the tool. Tools should never be the reason to hold an ideation session and that's often what happens.

A truly innovative culture, a culture that can fulfill the great promise of innovation, features a shared set of values that are practiced regularly. It's a mindset and commitment to innovation which includes integrating innovation into how employees are measured and recognized. It's about how creativity is supported. It includes developing a system of follow through to turn ideas into reality. It starts with ensuring that both employees and their ideas are valued.

I know what you're thinking, "I bought a book about innovation; I don't want another corporate culture lecture." I'm not going to give you one. I am saying that without a culture in place which fully supports innovation – the effort it requires, the sacrifices it demands, the process involved, the communication necessary – your attempts to innovate will go nowhere.

IDEO is a company specializing in design and innovation consulting. IDEO consistently ranks as one of the highest rated companies in the world when it comes to innovation.

I happened to be visiting the IDEO offices in Palo Alto, California on summer intern orientation day. Each intern was presented a giant orientation binder – it had to be 300 pages.

The interns groaned expecting this binder to be full of policies, rules, standards and practices, boring case studies and endless forms and exercises. They opened the binders and found all the pages blank! The guide leading the interns told them, "We want you to fill up these binders and tell us what you learn over the next few months and what we can do better."

Think about the power of that message: IDEO, world renown for its ability to generate creative ideas and innovate, was turning to its interns, yet-to-graduate 20-year-olds with limited experience, and asking them for ideas. IDEO knows that to get the most from its people it can't tell them everything; it can't force them to expect certain experiences or demand everyone solve every problem the same way. IDEO wants its employees to have their own experiences, come to their own conclusions, see problems through their own unique prism and then tell the company how it can improve. They won't use all those ideas, but they want all those ideas.

This respect for and belief in the ideas of all employees – even day-one, unpaid interns – represents one facet of the dynamic culture of innovation which exists at IDEO. Think of how many people with advanced degrees, a proven track record of success, and 20 years experience don't have their ideas similarly valued at the office?

IDEO has great tools to use toward innovation and understands culture takes center stage. Tools go nowhere if the culture isn't in place to support their use.

When I talk about an innovative culture, I'm talking about much more than the physical work space. I often find that when groups want to create an innovative culture, mistakenly, the first action taken is an adjustment to the physical work environment. Since this "physical environment" usually attracts the initial focus of a business attempting to innovate, I'll address it now.

The Physical Environment

Bean bag chairs, motivational posters and foosball tables do not equal an innovative culture. When I talk to groups who want to be more innovative, nine times out of 10 their thoughts go first to the physical environment and a felt need for what is known as an "innovation station."

An "innovation station," in general, is a room in an office set aside for employees to daydream and be provided with a space to think more creatively. The philosophy here being that by surrounding employees with Legos, crayons and comfy couches their imaginations will be magically sparked.

Businesses tend to lean toward this "solution" because it's easy. Building an "innovation station" takes no more effort than a trip to Office Depot, Toys R Us, and some petty cash. Though tempting to think you can buy innovation out of a catalogue, innovation will never be acquired that way. Creating a truly innovative culture where a business changes its mindset, commits to work on innovation daily, and sacrifices to achieve in that area requires more effort.

Companies erroneously think that the "innovation station" will send a strong message to employees about their commitment to innovation. Instead, an internal conflict develops within the mind of each employee. This conflict arises because everything else about their office's culture sits in direct opposition to the fun and playful attitude of the "innovation station."

Most office buildings are otherwise painted in muted colors, enforce strict dress codes, and impersonally cordon employees from each other in monotonous cubes. Into that sterile environment, management places a brightly colored room filled with toys.

Intended message by management: we support innovation!

Message received by employees: fun and creativity are limited to the new "innovation station," your desk is for real work.

When a business' culture doesn't support the idea of play as work, employees will avoid using the "innovation station" for fear of being thought of as slacking off or not working hard. It becomes perceived as a play room.

Why would anyone think a blue-collar worker with calluses on his hands or a white-collar worker in a power suit would feel comfortable working in a room sitting on a bar stool and staring at a Slinky while new-age music plays? It's out of order with everything else taking place at the location.

People can't flip a switch on their creativity. Employees' heads spin when they're encouraged to be playful and joke around in one room and in the next room, five feet away, that same behavior becomes utterly out of place and inappropriate.

I've been in offices that look more like dorm rooms with each cube a snapshot into the personality of the employee. I've found these companies to have a high level of creative and imaginative output. This output exists not because of the bobble-head dolls and snow globes found on desks, it's the fully engrained and supported message that innovation matters. Paired with that message is a complete integration of creative and imaginative behaviors into all areas of the business.

This doesn't mean that you can't have creativity and imagination in a more conservative business environment. A business can have taupe walls and cubes and be extremely creative and innovative as long as its culture supports and encourages the proper behaviors and mindset.

From my experience, the majority of "innovation stations" become de facto break rooms within months and inside a year have been converted back into cube space. Innovation doesn't magically happen because employees have access to "neat" stuff and comfortable furniture – if only it were that easy.

Here's the biggest problem with the "innovation station" philosophy: do you want to have an office, facility, or school where innovation happens in only one specially designated corner? Wouldn't it make more sense to support innovation everywhere, to encourage creativity in every location an employee works?

This one-spot focus of innovation mentality directly links to another misguided notion in the implementation of innovation. Innovation Day! Innovation Week! Innovation Month!

Today's Special: Innovation

Approaching innovation in such a limited scope communicates to employees that successful innovation can be achieved in an isolated time frame. For innovation to generate the results you expect, it has to be practiced regularly and everywhere. It can't be the focus of a single day or week or month or room.

If you want just one idea, by all means, "Innovation Day!" is for you. If, however, you're looking to establish an innovation pipeline that generates a consistent stream of results, innovation needs to be worked at every day.

Think of it like safety. The companies who prioritize safety don't hold a "Safety Day!" nor is there a "Safety Room." They make a commitment to be safe every day, everywhere and to reinforce its importance constantly to all employees. They continually think about safety and act on it.

The commitment extends beyond management. At the safest companies, employees take it upon themselves to enforce safe practices. If an employee at a company that values safety saw another employee placing a ladder on top of a chair balanced against a desk in order to change a light bulb, the other employee would stop him immediately and help find a safer way.

Innovation needs the same commitment. Innovation needs to be supported to the point where it becomes engrained in the thoughts and habits of all employees all the time.

Once employees have been conditioned to constantly be thinking about innovation you'll find engaging employees in the process of innovation to be one more reason why a focus on culture must come before the introduction of tools.

Employee Engagement

Successful innovation comes from employees. Their ideas will drive it. Their cumulative years of experience, relationships and knowledge of the product will result in the *imagination*, which sparks the *creativity* that develops *invention* and ultimately results in *innovation*.

For a business to tap into its people's brain power, it has to understand what motivates them. Most employees achieve their greatest potential when they have a positive relationship and trust with their manager. If a business refuses to address this relationship then its attempts at innovation will go nowhere.

People need jobs for the money, retirement and health insurance benefits, but no one wakes up early to go to work because of the great dental plan. An employee's relationship with his direct supervisor and the passive and negative, or active and positive, engagement experienced through that relationship determines an employee's level of productivity and commitment.

A truly innovative culture necessarily supports this relationship by fostering more open and respectful communication between employees and their manager or supervisor. Committing to innovation necessitates the commitment to a free-flowing exchange of ideas between team members and management.

As this communication becomes more regular and more open – and starts to deliver results – the process feeds itself as employees become more engaged in the company with their ideas being respected and put into action. At the same time, management builds a greater trust with employees and values their ideas as these ideas begin to benefit the company.

If a level of trust does not exist between employees and

managers, innovation lacks the fertile ground in which to grow. Creativity happens from the interplay and interaction of people's ideas and how they build upon each other. Without trust, no interaction occurs as individuals isolate themselves and their ideas.

When employees are worried about managers stealing their ideas and taking credit for them, ideas will be silenced and innovation goes nowhere. When employees are disillusioned about the introduction of innovation, having seen numerous other "management initiatives" come and go and be forgotten, a "this too shall pass" mentality takes hold and innovation goes nowhere. Worst of all, when employees have become hostile toward their company and ask themselves, "why should I give my ideas to the company to help them make more money," a "me vs. them" mentality has been created and key issues of trust must be addressed before expecting innovation to bear fruit.

Fully engaging employees in the process of innovation gives them an opportunity to take on new projects and responsibilities, to demonstrate leadership skills in small groups, build influencing and greater communication skills, to gain and give recognition, and provides grander purpose to their work. These are all behaviors any organization should desire its people to learn and demonstrate and they can all be achieved and practiced through small and progressively larger innovation projects. I continue to find a myriad of advantageous unintended benefits through my work with innovation.

During a business' introduction to the process of innovation, employees will talk to each other about it. The degree to which a company positively engages its employees in all aspects of the process will frame how those conversations sound.

Will employees be mocking and sabotaging the efforts or

actively promoting them and selling them to co-workers? A negative culture dismisses employees, who will in turn, dismiss innovation efforts. A culture featuring trust and respect receives employee support because it supports them.

Without a supportive culture, whether its safety, production, diversity or innovation, results won't be experienced.

If you were all fired up to implement innovation and base it on great tools, don't despair, we'll get to tools. Respect the abilities and ideas of employees, engage them in the process, and make a full commitment – that comes first.

How do you do all that? I'm glad you asked.

CHAPTER 4
Creating an Innovative Culture

A re you ready to get started?

I hope so because the remainder of this book details steps to be taken in order for your organization to realize the promise of innovation. As you continue reading it will be of great benefit for you to have in mind how you can put this information into action. This book serves as an innovation instruction manual; continually be thinking about how you can use its contents.

You now understand why the establishment of an innovative culture should be the first step to take in the innovation process. How do you do that?

First, let's make sure you know what I mean when I say "culture." Remember how I defined culture: a core set of values that become fully integrated and regularly practiced as behaviors within an organization – core values, fully integrated, regularly practiced as behaviors.

The core values you want to instill as the foundation of your innovative culture are: *communication*, *candor*, *curiosity* and *commitment*.

These values are long lasting and non-negotiable. They are not subject to market fluctuations or personnel changes. These values should define the way you operate. Your company's current CEO, where the Dow closed today or your last quarterly earnings report cannot alter them.

I'm not asking you to scrap your existing corporate culture and values and replace them. Your corporate culture has been long established and supported. I want you to add the values of *communication, candor, curiosity* and *commitment* to your current culture, or build them into your culture if you've yet to define it.

Merely having and stating values won't net you results until they are translated into behaviors – regularly practiced behaviors. Along with a deeper explanation of these values, I will provide you with examples of them in practice. Additionally, I will provide simple activities you can use to start training your people to exhibit those behaviors. They can then start to become ingrained in your culture.

COMMUNICATION

When establishing the values necessary for an innovative culture, there's a reason communication comes first. Most of the problems any group will have with innovation will be the result of poor communication, while most of the successes will have a foundation in strong communication. Success or failure won't be the result of tools, training or ideas; it will be determined by communication.

Has the importance of innovation been communicated clearly? Have the goals been well defined and understood by everyone? Has the role each employee is expected to play been set? Is feedback and follow up on ideas regular? Are team members encouraged to come forward with their ideas?

When these discussions and discussions like them take place

openly and consistently, results from innovation are almost sure to follow.

People already have ideas and don't need training or tools to spark them, they need focus, feedback, collaboration and support to shape those ideas into new products, services or efficiencies.

Candor, curiosity and *commitment*, the values which follow *communication,* are extensions and specific aspects of communication. Communication is the wellspring for all the values necessary to the innovative culture, without it, innovation can not flourish.

WHAT YOU CAN DO TODAY TO HAVE THE **COMMUNICATION** NEEDED TO CREATE AN INNOVATIVE CULTURE:

- Start building greater communication by sharing your belief in innovation with team members. Explain why you're starting on this path and innovation's importance to you and the group. Use this book to show your team all the exciting possibilities innovation holds for each of them individually and for the team as a whole.

- Begin to make conversations surrounding innovation a part of every meeting. Remember that to be innovative, innovative practices must become fully ingrained into a workplace and regularly practiced. If you have a weekly staff meeting, include this discussion. If you don't have regular meetings, show your people your commitment to innovation by calling them together and sharing your passion for the subject. Find ways to make sure you communicate that your passion hasn't waned as time goes on.

- Once you've expressed your passion and belief in innovation use Chapter 2 and share the definitions of *imagination*, *creativity*, *invention* and *innovation*. Make sure everyone is speaking the same language.

- Detail to employees the new behaviors you're expecting to see from them as a part of the innovative culture you are instituting. There's no reason to be mysterious about this. Inform team members that communication, candor, curiosity and commitment are what you will be recognizing and rewarding. Take that message a step further by specifying exactly what types of communication, candor, curiosity and commitment you're looking for.

- A more advanced form of communication includes gathering and sharing customer insights, what people hear going on in the marketplace, and opinions on how those changes will affect your business.

GOOD COMMUNICATION: Good communication begins when communication takes place. When people are talking, interacting, sharing ideas both internally and externally, up and down the food chain, good communication exists. When communication within your team is equitable with equal parts listening and talking you're on the right track.

Good communication exists long after an individual's specific contribution to the innovation process has passed. One of the best examples of this I've personally experienced took place with a team I was consulting on innovating new product ideas. Months after the initial brainstorming sessions were held and my role in the project was completed, I continued to receive periodic updates from the team leader about the progress of the initiative and where in the process the team was currently. This feedback made me feel more connected to the team and assured me that the work we had done was moving forward.

BAD COMMUNICATION: When communication becomes irregular, going through bursts and then long periods of inactivity, communication's power has been diminished.

When communication becomes isolated to cliques or takes place only on similar planes of status, the effectiveness of collaboration has been short-circuited by bad communication.

When communication becomes strictly scheduled – the monthly ideas meeting – communication is stifled with that meeting becoming the only time individuals communicate; for communication to blossom, it must be free of such constraints.

UGLY COMMUNICATION: A communication sin numerous managers and organizations commit entails asking for ideas and then not responding to the ideas received. Staff members encouraged to submit ideas and be creative while receiving no communication back from those who asked for the ideas exemplifies ugly communication. Asking people for ideas and not acknowledging receipt of those ideas will derail future idea generation campaigns.

I once spoke with an employee who had more than 20 years of experience at his facility. We were talking about idea generation and he told me he hadn't submitted an idea in years. I asked him, "Why not?" He said he submitted a number of ideas several years ago and never heard anything back; he didn't even know if they were read.

Here was a long-time employee with ideas who wanted to share them, but his site's communication loop was in such an ugly condition there was no system in place to let this employee know if his idea was even received.

Why would this person continue to submit ideas into a perceived black hole? When locations or teams complain about a lack of ideas, most often it's not a process or tools problem, it's a communication problem.

You may find you're not receiving ideas because you're not communicating effectively. Communication is a two-way loop. When you ask contributors for input, you must be prepared to provide feedback.

"When we don't get a response from someone, we imagine one, and it sounds something like this: 'Terrible job you did the other day. And, oh, by the way, I don't like you very much,'" Peter Bregman, writing on Harvard Business Review online.

<u>CANDOR</u>

As a team's communication improves and a culture of innovation starts taking hold, hundreds of ideas will be received, most of which can not be used. An innovative culture opens minds and results in a powerful flow of ideas. To manage that flow, keep one word in mind: "candor."

Most of us are good with praise, some of us have even mastered admonishment, but how many of us excel at candor? Few people are able to receive an idea that isn't useful and honestly communicate with the giver why the idea doesn't work in a way that supports, encourages, and keeps that employee engaged and generating ideas.

When we present an idea, we make ourselves vulnerable. It's risky. Our idea could be rejected. No one enjoys rejection.

When someone steps forward to present an idea, they are demonstrating that they care enough about the team or company or challenge to risk rejection – those are the employee's business needs. For employees to feel comfortable presenting ideas, they have to be assured their ideas will be respected and considered, even when rejected. An innovative culture respects all ideas and the employees who generate them while at the same time being candid about their usefulness.

Candor includes coaching and meaningful feedback. If an idea isn't useful, explain why not. How could the idea be shaped to become more useful? Does the idea need to be explained more clearly to be understood? Is there a piece of the idea that is useful and could be developed? Is there a different problem you'd like the idea generator to concentrate on?

An idea should never be met with a flat "no." Candor means more than an ability to say "no," it means an ability to say "no" while being constructive and helpful in providing the giver the feedback necessary so his next idea gets a "yes."

When you and your sweetheart are thinking about going out for dinner, how does the conversation start? You ask her where she wants to go, right? She says, "Hunan House." You don't have a taste for Chinese food. How do you respond? "No." "NO!" "I HATE Chinese food!" "That's a dumb idea." Of course not – not unless you want to eat alone.

Instead, you provide candid feedback that is working toward a solution to the "Where to eat" question. "I don't have a taste for Chinese food tonight sweetie-pie, what about pizza?"

"I had pizza at work yesterday," she says, "how about Burger Joe's?" You candidly reply, "A burger sounds good, but Burger Joe's is kind of far away, I don't think we'd be able to make the movie if we went there; what about something closer?"

"Well then How about Burger Mike's?"

"Oh yeah, that sounds great."

Candid communication features an open and respectful exchange of ideas which provides feedback on how to shape thoughts into solutions. It works for dinner, it works for innovation.

WHAT YOU CAN DO TODAY TO HAVE THE **CANDOR** NEEDED TO CREATE AN INNOVATIVE CULTURE:

- Set clear expectations and let people know all of their ideas aren't going to be used. Make equally clear that unused ideas aren't bad or stupid. Reinforce that you want ideas and continually remind employees not to be offended if theirs don't get implemented. Tell your people that a continued willingness to present ideas will put them in greater esteem in your eyes.
- Establish a mindset that thinks of all feedback as a gift. Remind team members that any feedback given is presented with the goal of making the idea better.
- Condition employees not to become defensive when ideas are questioned. Replace defensiveness with questions such as, "why wouldn't you use it" or "what would make you use this?" Every great author has an editor. The editor does his job when he suggests changes and makes cuts.
- Present ideas, don't sell them. In a sense, you want your prototype to fail. You want to know what's wrong with it so it can be improved. That philosophy comes through candid communication and must be established and reinforced since it's contrary to the way most of us think.

- Challenge your team to change the way it thinks about ideas and criticism. Establish less of a personal connection to ideas by reminding individuals that almost no ideas are perfect out of the gate. Only through candid communication with each other, where feedback is treated as a gift, can we make our ideas the best they can be and most useful.

GOOD CANDOR: Candor needs to be respectful, appreciative, honest and delivered in a timely fashion. It should be specific, actionable, open and constructive. A good use of candor doesn't slam ideas; it enhances them and shapes them. If you want employees to take the time to submit their ideas, then you have to take the time to consider those ideas and return your candid feedback.

BAD CANDOR: "I like it." This response to an idea drives me crazy, along with its twin, "that's fine." "I like it" and "that's fine" don't help anyone because they are not specific or useful. Unfortunately they are the most common feedback responses. People are too polite and chances are they don't like the idea and are only saying they do to avoid any uncomfortable exchanges.

When someone tells me, "I like it," I immediately ask them, "Tell me what you like." "Tell me how you would improve it." "What would you change?" Their responses to those questions can be useful.

Bad candor is vague and "I like it" is incredibly vague.

A demonstration of how meaningless "I like it" has become can be found in a recent customer survey analysis I came across. Customers were asked to grade a company on a one to five scale with "5" being considered a "superior" product, "4" being "I liked it," on down to "1" which was "strongly disliked."

The survey results found the vast majority of customers ranked the business a "4" out of "5." With that strong of a ranking, the company couldn't understand why it wasn't seeing more repeat business. The survey company went back to the customers they previously questioned and upon further examination found that those who stated they "liked" the product, rating it a seemingly impressive "4" out of "5," were less than 50% likely to buy their product.

In our incredibly sensitive culture, "I like it" has become a catch-all for anything between "I love it" and "I hate it." There's a lot of room between love and hate and "like" doesn't come close to defining it all.

UGLY CANDOR: Ugly candor becomes personal. Ugly candor dismisses ideas out of hand. Ugly candor includes phrases like: "Your idea makes no sense," "Could we get serious here," "Could we have some good ideas for once," "That'll never work."

Ugly candor is sweeping, negative, kneejerk, and based on absolutes. I have seen groups nearly come to blows following the use and receipt of ugly candor. Remember, we attach great personal pride to our ideas. When those ideas are rejected, we feel rejected. Keep that in mind when using candor.

"A 'No' uttered from deepest conviction is better and greater than a 'Yes' merely uttered to please, or what is worse, to avoid trouble." Mahatma Gandhi

CURIOSITY

How does your team need to be more like a 5-year-old?

CREATING AN INNOVATIVE CULTURE

Afternoon naps may help; continually asking "why" will help.

If you've spent any time around children, you know what it's like to be peppered with "why." "Why does mommy have to go to work?" "Why are dogs bigger than cats?" "Why do I have to go to bed now?"

An equally curious mindset by employees has a powerful impact.

A philosophy of "why" will lead to conversations that create a culture where everything can be challenged and looked at to be improved. Employees routinely questioning the status quo, questioning processes, asking themselves and others about why things are done the way they are done, or why different approaches haven't been tried, often lead to revealing discussions. These discussions pave the way for breakthroughs in improving those processes and approaches.

Imagine the type of conversations that could be had and the engagement and relationships which could be built if questions were responded to with enthusiasm and appreciation instead of dismissal and a mindset of being bothered by them. When curiosity intersects with candor and communication, knowledge is gained, ideas blossom and solutions arise.

In conjunction with "why" is "how." "How does this work?" "How does what I do affect others?"

Finding these answers helps people become experts. Curiosity leads to a better understanding of processes, customers, and technology and this will lead to better ideation sessions through greater employee insight and comprehension. The better someone understands something, the better ideas they'll have regarding it. When an employee asks a question, that employee demonstrates that he cares enough about the company to ask questions to gain more knowledge in the hope of being able to better serve the team.

Any business should want its employees to be interested in all parts of the business, not just their specific role. Employees should realize what they do impacts others upstream and down. They should, with practice, start to see parallels to other jobs and processes which will lead to even more unique ideas.

I once visited a processing plant were I walked through the facility asking line employees which products – brand names – they produced? Not one employee could tell me. Here was a group of 800 employees so disinterested about any part of the business other than the incredibly specific job they performed each day that they couldn't even go to a grocery store and buy the product they put out for certain. Wouldn't it seem natural to want to know that? Imagine the increase in sales if just the employees at that facility started exclusively buying the brands they produced.

Those employees had been conditioned not to ask questions.

As a result of this observation, the company's management almost immediately instituted new practices aimed at educating employees and encouraging them to be proactive in asking questions. Two years later I returned to this same facility and took a similar employee survey. The results were the opposite with most employees being able to inform me not only about the products they produced, but a wide variety of other processes and practices at the location separate of their specific job.

For curiosity to be most effective, it must work both ways. It should come from employees up to management and from management on down. Don't forget that employees are also consumers. They make choices every day that lead them to use the products and services you are working to improve. That's where your market research should begin. You will be surprised by the insights your employees have regarding your products and services.

This reminds me of the stories we all heard in the 1980s coming out of Detroit where the GM, Ford or Chrysler employee drove his Toyota or Honda to the plant and was accosted by management and coworkers for not buying the car he helped build. Instead of tormenting these employees, wouldn't it have made more sense for "Big Three" management and employees to ask the foreign car drivers why they bought a product that competes directly with the one they are producing – a decision that could conceivably cost them their job? The "Big Three" were not acting with curiosity.

Years later General Motors would reverse its thinking by inviting a group of self-described "Chevy Haters" – consumers determined never to buy a Chevy – to provide input and feedback through the development process of its Volt model.

WHAT YOU CAN DO TODAY TO FOSTER THE **CURIOSITY** NEEDED TO CREATE AN INNOVATIVE CULTURE:

- Ask questions of your team members and the people around you. Let people know you are looking for questions.
- You need to communicate the new expected behavior of curiosity. Similar to communication and candor, inform team members that you are expecting curiosity from them and will be rewarding it.
- Investigate. Asking questions comes first. From this initial step springs a curiosity about wide ranging aspects of your job and industry. What are my competitors doing? What are best practices from other companies, or teams within my company, that I could be using? What new technology is

on the horizon? How are my customers' needs changing?

- Progressively investigating wider spheres of influence broadens an individual's perspective and understanding and leads to better idea generation. Regularly demonstrating this more advanced form of curiosity allows you to gain knowledge and reinforces its importance to employees.

GOOD CURIOSITY: A person with curiosity, going out of his way to investigate, follow up and explore an issue, then bringing his insights and questions to the attention of others. Curiosity is active and shared. This type of unsolicited curiosity should be the goal of innovative teams.

To reach that level, start asking questions.

When I was in school, every day as soon as I got home my mom asked what new thing I learned. I knew that question was coming so I had to be prepared with an answer. "Nothing" or "I don't know" were unacceptable responses.

Having to answer that question made me look at school differently; it made me consider what I was learning instead of having it just wash over me. It forced me to fully comprehend the lessons so I could explain and share them with my mom. Even though my mom knew long division and what happened at D-Day, she wanted to make sure I understood what I was learning well enough to communicate the concepts to another person.

Regularly asking your team members about what they're learning or observing or experiencing will start them questioning, investigating and communicating more effectively.

BAD CURIOSITY: When only one person asks questions or takes it upon himself to challenge the group while everyone else sits silently, a culture of curiosity doesn't exist. When one person takes the initiative to posses all necessary information, curiosity becomes stifled. This prevents them from learning anything new.

No business, company, or team should ever rely on one person for all its know-how and information. Establishing a culture of curiosity prevents that from happening.

UGLY CURIOSITY: "I don't know." "I don't care." "You don't need to know that." "That's the way we've always done it." "Because." "That's not important." "That's none of your business."

Hopefully you'll never hear those responses again. They need to be eliminated from your vocabulary as they are the classic enemies of curiosity. If you as a team leader expect curiosity from employees you have to reward people with an answer. You don't need to have all the answers, you don't have to reveal company secrets or share personal or potentially embarrassing information, but you have to respect the act of asking questions and want to help people find the answers.

"I have no special talents. I am only passionately curious."
Albert Einstein

COMMITMENT

There are two separate types of commitment in innovation. First, a broad scale commitment to innovation as a way of doing business must be established. Companies, teams, team leaders and individuals need to be committed to the belief that the use of a proven process of innovation can lead them to the achievement of their goals. Secondly, a narrower commitment from individuals to specific innovation projects and their role in those projects is required. An employee must commit to performing his assigned task to the best of his ability.

Both of these commitments are attained the same way, through passion.

A passion for innovation as a way of doing business and a commitment to its practice can be instituted simply by communicating its wide array of benefits to individuals. Explain to employees how the adoption of innovative practices will enrich their work lives through greater employee engagement, communication and creative opportunities.

The best way of receiving a commitment from team members to specific innovation projects comes by finding what they are passionate about and allowing them to explore opportunities in those areas. When you identify a role each individual can embrace, excel at and feel comfortable with, that effort will be returned to you as *commitment*.

Most innovation books and speeches invariably feature the mantra: "Everyone can innovate." More accurately, I say, "everyone has a role to play in the process of innovation." Many people don't see a role for themselves so you want to encourage employees to look for ways of becoming involved.

If an employee isn't part of idea generation, can he be part of the evaluation or feedback stages which help those ideas become better? Could he assist in the building, testing or refining of prototypes? What about a position in project management or market research of the idea being developed? There are dozens of ways to involve people in innovation and anything that encourages them to feel an ownership of the process through their contribution will draw out their passion and create a commitment.

Committing to the process of innovation comes easy when the idea is yours; the best companies find ways to secure the commitment of all employees to the process even when their ideas are not the ones being used.

I will always remember an innovation class I held where during the first bathroom break one of the participants frankly told me she couldn't understand why she was attending. The woman said flatly that she was not innovative; she was simply not an idea person.

I asked her what she did best. Without hesitation she told me she, "I get things done." Give her a task and she'll hammer it out.

I immediately informed her that she was as innovative as anyone in the group.

I can still picture the surprise on her face as that was the last thing she expected to hear. I believe she was hoping I'd excuse her from the workshop after she revealed her shortcomings in the arena of idea generation. Not a chance.

I reminded this employee of the definition of "innovation:" the end result – when a value from imagination, creativity and invention has been realized.

Idea generation is a critical step in the innovation process, but until those ideas are developed into new products, services or process improvements that generate results – often through the work of separate action-oriented people like her – they're only ideas, not innovations.

Explaining the role of action-oriented employees to the innovation process provided this previously disaffected team member a place to commit. She was instantly energized by finding a role to play and a role she could excel at. As the class moved forward and out of the idea generation phase into discussions regarding proto-types, time frames, costs and logistics, not only did this employee no longer drift on the edges of the group, she enthusiastically took center stage spearheading conversations in areas where her talents were required.

Embrace and utilize the distinct abilities of employees because almost no one can carry the burden of innovation singularly. A widely held misconception surrounding innovation envisions it as the exclusive realm of the "Lone Genius," brilliantly imagina-tive thinkers like Di Vinci, Franklin and Edison. Nothing could be further from the truth. Most innovations are not the result of geniuses working isolated in futuristic labs like the scientist in "Back to the Future" who built a time machine from a DeLorean. Far more prevalent are the thousands of innovations developed by teams of regular people following a coordinated, collaborative process of innovation.

I'm imaginative and creative, but when it comes to follow through and action, I always seem to find another idea to distract me from completion of the first idea. The woman I've described was unable to formulate new and different ideas, but was expert at taking the ideas of others and making them a reality. Separately, neither of us are innovators, working together we both are.

To ensure employee commitment to innovation, as well as results, a one-size-fits-all philosophy regarding roles and respon-sibilities will not work. Everyone has a part in the "movie" of innovation however everyone's part is not the same. A movie fea-tures more than a leading man or woman. A great movie needs a supporting cast, extras, a producer, a director, a sound man, costume designers, set designers, a script writer, someone to scout locations and receive the permission of local officials to film there, gaffers, catering, editors, and marketing. Innovation, like a movie, requires a wide variety of individuals possessing a wide variety of skills committed to an equally wide variety of responsibilities to succeed. This critical understanding differs from much of the current thought on innovation.

Innovation soars when you find people's strengths and maximize them.

WHAT YOU CAN DO TODAY TO DEVELOP THE **COMMITTMENT** NEEDED TO CREATE AN INNOVATIVE CULTURE:

- Examine your team. Without typecasting or relying on current positions determine who would fit into one of these four categories:
- A problem identifier. An employee who sees the big picture, potential issues and concerns, and often recognizes opportunities in the marketplace long before others. These employees help lead the way to unimagined growth.
- Idea person. This individual thinks differently and always seems to have ideas and solutions for questions or problems.
- Editor. Editors are often seen as negative and always seem to find the problems, pitfalls and details with projects and proposals few others can. This person exists in a practical, not theoretical, world and talks about what can be done, not what could or should be done. This employee provides candid feedback and can shape ideas.
- Action person. This employee makes things happen. They have the ability to take ideas and turn them into products and services which can be profited from.

By understanding employees' strengths in the different aspects of innovation you'll be able to better assign roles, put complete and diverse teams together and optimize the talents of the people you're presently working with. This assessment may expose an area of weakness you didn't realize your team had or reveal unnecessary redundancies.

Going through this process can provide the opportunity to dig deeper into your employees' abilities. Try presenting your people different tasks in the process of innovation and see how they handle them. Ask people what their passions are and where they see themselves fitting along this scale.

GOOD COMMITMENT: When people are working collaboratively and "cross functionally" on innovation projects good commitment exists. When everyone understands their role and embraces it, and the role they serve is the one best suited to them, you will experience a strong commitment. Where leaders and managers allow and direct employees to play to their strengths, commitment is sure.

BAD COMMITMENT: The "Lone Genius." One person working in isolation on all aspects of a project or idea will destroy a broader commitment from the majority of employees, to the project specifically, and innovation's practice in general. When one individual dominates the process, other team members become disinterested and use the "Lone Genius" as an excuse to disconnect believing that "someone else will take care of it."

"Lone Geniuses" working independently often become overly possessive or secretive about their ideas, struggles or progress thereby discouraging them to accept candid feedback. This derails communication and collaboration.

Additionally, the "Lone Genius" often holds his own interests above those of the company and the group which becomes overly dependent on this individual as he assumes more and more responsibility and ownership of projects. The risks and dangers inherit here need not be expounded on.

UGLY COMMITMENT: Forcing people into areas or responsibilities they are uncomfortable with corrodes commitment. Employees pushed into roles which make them uncomfortable create a dread of the process, holds back the rest of the group, and fails to capitalize on individual strengths.

We've all seen this in action with the placing of a team of people around a table where the manager then directs each and every one of them to present an idea. Here's what happens.

The "idea person" has six ideas, loves them all and hates having to swallow the five he can't submit. The "editor" had an idea, but his focus has shifted to the problems he sees with the idea the "idea person" put forward. The "action person" is silent and has broken into a sweat because he doesn't have any ideas and gets nervous speaking before a group. The "problem identifier" finds the entire exercise a waste of time because the ideas so far presented are not focused on the biggest problem he sees the group facing.

None of the employees yet to share their idea are concentrating on the individual speaking because they're worried about their idea not sounding smart.

The "idea person" now goes nuts because he just thought of another idea better than the one he used already.

"Action person" is starting to get a queasy stomach because he really doesn't have an idea and thinks his voice sounds squeaky.

"Editor" doesn't understand how the previous idea could ever be delivered to the marketplace.

"Problem identifier" just gave his idea and now turns his attention to lunch, and the manager wonders why his attempt at idea generation didn't yield better results.

Everyone ends up unsatisfied because they were all forced to contribute in the same way regardless of what their individual talents are. Embrace and apply the unique skills and experiences of your team members to create the commitment and realize the results you're looking for.

"It seems safe to say that significant discovery, really creative thinking, does not occur with regard to problems about which the thinker is lukewarm." Mary Henle

Communication, candor, curiosity and commitment, by establishing these values you will be well on your way to experiencing the potentially dramatic results achievable through innovation. If you resolve to opening communication, practicing candor, encouraging curiosity and developing commitment, your attempts at innovation will take off.

CHAPTER 5
Sucpectnition
(Success + Expectations + Recognition)

Communication, candor, curiosity and commitment are the values being established and you want those values translated into behaviors from your people. In order for your team to start demonstrating those behaviors, it has to buy in to the values as important and necessary.

How do you achieve that? You achieve that through success.

How do you succeed? You succeed by first attempting small innovation projects, managing your expectations and recognizing a job well done – that's "suspectnition".

Nothing Breeds Success Like Success

Early in the Civil War, legendary Confederate general Robert E. Lee was derisively nicknamed "Granny Lee" by his troops for his timid style. After a string of stunning victories "Granny" was dropped and those same soldiers began jumping at Lee's every directive.

Lee's success, which was Lee's army's success, created a total belief in his abilities and commands because his men experienced them working. Success created buy-in for Lee and it will have the same impact on your team's innovation efforts.

If you're willing to practice and be patient you will achieve the successes which result in a committed use of the process of innovation from your team.

Expectations

Imagine yourself as a baby.

What if your parents stood you up at nine-months-old and said, "Walk." Further imagine that when you toppled over, they threw up their hands and said, "I guess we don't have a walker, I wonder what else he can do?"

Fortunately, parents have more patience and lower expectations. Your parents stood you up time and time and time again. They held your hands and walked behind you so you only had to move your legs. They encouraged you when you tried and failed and applauded your attempts to keep going.

When you finally succeeded they were overjoyed. When you wobbled from the sofa to the end table, pictures were taken, grandparents were called, times and dates were written down – it was a huge success. Your first steps!

Fast forward 12 years and your parents are no longer calling aunts and uncles when you walk from the bathroom to the kitchen because the bar has been raised. The bar was raised gradually though and milestones along the way were recognized and celebrated.

After you first began walking and became more comfortable with it, you started to run. That's a success. You weren't competing for the Olympic 100 meter championship, but you were running – faster and faster all the time.

Then you started to apply your walking and running – and jumping! – to games. You played catch in the yard or shot baskets in the driveway. You weren't on a team, you weren't competing, but you were making progress and achievements were recognized – juggling a soccer ball, throwing a spiral, hitting a ball off the batting cage machine.

As time passed, you became more and more skilled and advanced. You joined a team, began competing and applying the skills you'd developed over the years in ways you never could have initially. You were sprinting, doing cartwheels, hitting curveballs and walking on your hands. It all started with your first steps.

The same progression will be experienced with innovation. An early focus on the basics and small steps develops the foundation for greater success in the future.

Start by looking for opportunities to try. Begin with holding ideation sessions surrounding small-scope issues: how can your recycling program be improved, what community activities or charities would you like the group to become involved in, where should the holiday party be held, personal goals for next year, etc.

Celebrate the completion of those tasks, they are victories. Try and try again with progressively greater goals in mind. Examine your results, recognize them and try again.

This demands patience and the initial results may not seem monumental, but if you want to transform your business and become recognized as innovative, you have to start small. By continuing to practice and set realistic expectations you will create the successes necessary for your group to buy into the values of innovation and practice the behaviors you're seeking.

As you aim bigger and continue to experience success, you will find your team pushing you to do even more. You'll start by standing up, you'll advance to walking, eventually you'll be running and from there the possibilities are limitless.

Recognition

Recognition plays a critical role in this progression.

Recall Doug from Ft. Collins. Doug refused to introduce a process of innovation because he wasn't measured on it; he was measured on production and safety. As much as Doug was only measured on production and safety, he was also only recognized for production and safety.

He was not recognized for innovation. His recognition was a prize for man hours worked without an accident. That recognition and measurement created a focus.

I previously addressed key drivers of employee engagement. The relationship between an employee and his direct supervisor is the top driver of employee engagement and recognition joins it in the top-three.

Everyone likes to be recognized for a job well done. Recognition feels good. Before concerning yourself with how to measure success, concentrate first on recognizing success. Measurement can come later as you become more advanced with your innovation goals and experience, for starters, go out of your way to recognize success.

Begin incorporating recognition of successes in innovation and idea generation into the recognition programs you already have. If none exist, create them. There are any number of ways to do this: "most candid communicator," "best demonstration of curiosity," "greatest commitment to innovation."

The most effective innovation team leaders and managers are aware of, thank, and congratulate employees daily for their contribution to innovation efforts in all aspects of the process from curiosity to follow-through, communication, leadership, brainstorming – anything. Leaders who value innovation recognize it in action and go out of their way to applaud it the way leaders who value safety or productivity recognize and applaud them.

More than simply common courtesy and a demonstration of respect, this regular and informal recognition supports high levels of employee engagement and creates a positive, affirmative work environment. I've found the long term effects of such daily praise far more beneficial than once-a-year recognition at the company picnic.

A pitfall to avoid with recognition comes through the establishment of a financial reward system for idea generation. You have a lot to learn about the innovation process and groups or businesses trying it for the first time have no idea what the results will be in the early stages. Hold off promising bonuses until you actually start to see measurable results.

In general, exchanging money for ideas doesn't work. Money can be a great motivator though its impact exists only in the short term and it's also been found to limit the number and quality of ideas submitted. When money is on the line, people tend to become more reserved. They're more likely to hold back and only share the ideas they feel will be deserving of the monetary reward. Employees essentially create an internal filtering process that eliminates many ideas before they have a chance to be reviewed by others and then potentially enhanced.

Another adverse side effect to awarding money or other

fantastic prizes for ideas is that when great prizes are on the line, employees focus on the prize and not the process or the ideas.

If you're awarding $5,000 for the most "innovative" idea, employees' attention will be centered on how great it would be to win that five-grand and what they could do with the money. Their motivation for submitting ideas will be to pay credit card bills or take a trip to Vegas, not design a better product, cut waste or answer whatever specific problem has been asked.

Team member focus should be on the challenge, the customer need, the idea requested. Money and prizes distract from the purpose of idea generation which is to develop better ideas, not win stuff.

The idea of awarding a "grand prize" for "best idea" works just as poorly. Rewarding one person means that everyone else lost and as I've demonstrated earlier a collaborative approach to innovation achieves the best results.

Establishing internal competition and the conflict that will develop from it, the inevitable squabbles over who won and why, and the fact most great ideas aren't great out of the chute, only becoming great after collaboration and shaping, are a few of the reasons why an award system singling out individual ideas acts counterproductive to its purpose.

As you implement your innovative culture, recognize and encourage the behaviors, not the results. Once you become more experienced at innovation, you can determine how you want to reward results; to start with, focus on recognizing the behaviors. Good behaviors done repeatedly and consistently will give you the results you desire.

If you put this book down right now, never pick it up again, or never apply any of the creativity tools I'm about to present, but simply enact and regularly reinforce the values and ideas I've given you about an innovative culture, your team's innovation efforts will see a marked improvement.

Creating an innovative culture proves to be easier than it sounds. It requires no additional dollars or outside experts and can begin being put into place today. The values and behaviors necessary are scalable to the smallest groups or the largest companies and once that culture exists, you are ready for the introduction of creativity tools.

PART III

Tools and Techniques

"Studies have shown that creativity is close to 80 percent learned and acquired. We found that it's like exercising your muscles -- if you engage in the actions you build the skills."

Hal Gregersen, professor at Insead, as quoted by CNN.

CHAPTER 6
What is Your Goal?

Once a culture of innovation has been put in place you are now ready to start idea generation. The question again, "Where to start?"

There are countless tools and techniques to help you generate ideas and wading through them all to find the right one for your group and your challenge seems incredibly daunting. Like everything else, idea generation can be as complicated as you want to make it and I want to make it simple by focusing on the basics. When you master the basics and regularly practice the fundamentals, your brainstorming potential becomes unlimited.

Before selecting which tools you want to use to boost your brainstorming efforts, you first need to undertake an honest evaluation of the issues you are experiencing with your current idea generation efforts. Problems come first then tools are found to solve them.

If you see a nail sticking out of a board on your deck, that's a problem, so you go into your garage to find a hammer, a tool, to fix that problem. That nail presents a unique problem and the hammer is a tool specially designed to solve it. You've also got a drill in your garage and you could use the butt of that drill to pound the nail in, but that's not what it's designed for and while it might work, it won't work very well and it won't work for long.

The drill is a good tool, it's not a tool best suited to solve the problem of a nail sticking up. Creativity tools work the same way. There are different tools for different challenges and if you don't know what your shortcomings are, how can you pick the proper tools to address them? I will provide you tools designed to solve particular idea generation obstacles; you need to properly identify your team's obstacle.

While there are millions of individual business problems, I've found after working for more than a decade with tens of thousands of people around the globe in widely varied businesses that everyone's idea generation difficulties can be bucketed into one of three broad categories:

1. A need to increase the number of ideas
2. A need to improve the quality of ideas
3. A need to break through to a different way of thinking

My experience has also shown me that no single tool can effectively address each of these challenges simultaneously; there is no Swiss Army Knife of creativity tools. For each of these challenges, there are specific tools available to solve them. Actually, there are about 100 tools available to solve them; I'm going to give you the essential few necessary so you can start overcoming your difficulties today.

This approach marks a significant departure from the current thought in idea generation which continues to focus on tools before problems and continues to believe all tools apply to all situations.

I have worked with numerous groups who became enamored with a tool before understanding their brainstorming obstacle. More often than not I find the tool they're using mismatched to the team and challenge. When I attempt to present these teams a different tool better constructed to meet their individual situation, I'm generally met with resistance. They have devoted so much time and energy to learning that one tool and they believe it has to be able to work for them because they're so invested in it. When all you have is a hammer, every problem starts to look like a nail.

Watching these groups struggle to overcome their idea generation problems with unsuitable creativity tools spurred me to design better tools and better ideation sessions based on distinct goals and people. It also made clear to me the importance of identifying idea generation challenges before the selection of tools.

Increasing the number of ideas, improving the quality of ideas and *breaking through to a new way of thinking*, all three may be results you desire from your idea generation sessions, so how do you know which to choose?

First, understand that the tools designed to address each challenge are separate and that they progressively build upon each other. In general, your starting place will be determined by your level of experience with idea generation. If you're new to this process I'd strongly encourage you starting with *increasing the number of ideas*, in fact, it's a necessity.

Unless your team has extensive experience – and success – developing new ideas through brainstorming, you should focus your initial efforts on *increasing the number of ideas*. People ask me all the time why they can't skip the *increase the number of ideas* step and advance straight to *improving the quality of ideas*.

The reason is because the tools and techniques that lead to better ideas are built off those designed to generate more ideas and their application is only successful if you've mastered and practiced the exercises which precede them. The same holds true for *improving the quality of ideas* and *breaking through to a new way of thinking*.

View these idea generation challenges as a pyramid with *increasing the number of ideas* being the base, *improving the quality of ideas* being the middle, and *breaking through to a new way of thinking* the top. If you neglect any of the initial steps, your foundation will be weak and your pyramid will fall.

My approach to idea generation is unique because I'm not concerned with the specific business problem you're attempting to solve. To overcome your idea generation obstacles, it doesn't matter if you're trying to sell more pizzas, develop an electric car, or cut your water bill. What matters, and what you need to determine, are the results you're presently experiencing from your ideation sessions.

What are your struggles, what have your successes been, where are your breakdowns coming? Understanding your results allows you to identify your shortcomings and then chose the tools and techniques necessary to address them.

I'd love to be able to talk to you individually about your idea generation barriers and recommend the appropriate tool to overcome it, unfortunately my clones are still in the prototype phase. In the meantime, why don't you eavesdrop on a conversation I've had with dozens of managers looking for help maximizing their brainstorming by overcoming idea generation roadblocks. I'm sure you'll find yourself and your team in one of these conservations and that way, if we do get to talk, we can go straight to celebrity gossip.

Scenario 1

Me: "Mike Dugan here."

Jill: "Hey Mike, I need your help. We're working with Larry's Widgets around their new sustainability line. We've done some brainstorming, but we're just not coming up with good ideas. Larry's competition is hammering him with their Eco-Widget and Larry wants to catch up, but we're stuck."

Jill, like you and all of the people I've helped to supercharge their brainstorming sessions, understands what end result she wants out of her idea generation. She knows the specific business problem she wants solved – developing a product for Larry's Widgets "sustainability line" which can compete with the competitor's Eco-Widget –she doesn't know the roadblock preventing her team from attaining that result. The answer will be revealed after just one question from me.

Me: "All right Jill, what results have you experienced from the brainstorming sessions you've held so far?"

Jill: "Well, I've had some informal conversations with employees and other managers about some ideas and I've discussed a few possibilities with the customer, but I've found only a handful worth pursuing and nothing's really going anywhere. The brainstorming sessions I have held aren't generating the number or type of ideas I was expecting."

This response reminds me of the Linus Pauling quote, "The best way to get a great idea is to have a lot of ideas."

Jill recognizes that she needs a greater volume of ideas to

choose from in order to put some life into Larry's Widgets new sustainability line. Creatively, Jill needs to get the ball rolling, start people thinking, create some successes by putting tangible results on the board. Jill's team needs to *increase the number of ideas*.

These initial ideas don't have to be breakthroughs or final solutions and almost certainly won't be. That's to be expected. Becoming skilled in idea generation takes time and results may seem unspectacular at the beginning.

Many people approach brainstorming as a quest to find the "one" idea. From the start, they want the Holy Grail, a bull's-eye with their first shot. This mindset is unrealistic and will cause frustration. Thinking that way is tantamount to going into a large pitch-black room with a pen light looking for a dime. What are your chances of finding it? Tiny. You find the dime by flipping the switch and flooding the room with light. Put light everywhere, even places where you don't end up finding the dime.

HELPFUL HINT: Teams in need of *increasing the number of ideas* have often relied on suggestion boxes, open questions to employees or idea campaigns to drive results. This passive, shotgun approach to idea generation loses the power of focused and collaborative efforts. Relying on individuals working isolated from each other to solve problems and withholding from them the inherent power that comes from the strength of a group communicating rarely yields results superior to what teamwork can achieve.

Suggestion boxes are a particular pet peeve of mine. I describe them as the black hole of ideas. You're much more likely to find a gum wrapper in a suggestion box than a great idea fit to solve your unique business problems.

There are numerous reasons for this.

Suggestion boxes are almost never managed well; rarely are resources ever put behind their use or into the ideas submitted in order to explore how beneficial they might be. A feature that should be mandatory when ideas are requested and offered that I've yet to see incorporated into a suggestion box is a strong communication loop to update employees on the progress of their idea, or if it's even been read. The Grand Canyon could be filled with the ideas which have been submitted to suggestion boxes and have failed to generate any response back to the employee about the quality or usefulness of the idea - or even a, "thanks for the effort."

Suggestion boxes are horribly unfocused, failing to ask anything specific. You may need to cut your company's fuel consumption yet what you'll most likely find in the "Suggestion Box" are opinions on the cafeteria food and dirty jokes.

The effectiveness of suggestion boxes are further derailed by the biases of the person tasked to read them. What if a new process idea comes in that isn't on the radar screen of the employee sorting through the paper scraps or it's something he or she doesn't understand? It gets tossed.

Take my word after having spoken to hundreds of people around the world regarding their similar frustrations with suggestion boxes – they're useless. The characteristic shortcomings of suggestion boxes work to discourage employee engagement and create a de-motivating experience which tunes people out of the creative process.

Concentrating on *increasing the number of ideas* begins conditioning your people to start thinking critically and as problem solvers; establish a free exchange of ideas featuring candor and curiosity and see what develops.

Scenario 2

The next most frequent conversation I have with managers struggling at idea generation features a different answer to my question.

Me: "All right Jill, what results have you been getting from the brainstorming sessions you've held so far?"

Jill: "We're generating a lot of ideas, but we're not developing the really good breakthrough ideas we need and our customer expects. Brainstorming sessions are going well, we've had some successes, but I sense a rut developing. We could use a shake-up, something to spark us to that next-level solution."

When Jill's team has practiced the fundamental brainstorming tools, regularly produces a strong volume of ideas, and now finds itself struggling to produce the standout ideas necessary to achieve her specific innovation goal, her need has become *increasing the quality of ideas*.

Groups who have tried and advanced beyond the rudimentary brainstorming principles often experience this difficulty. These teams hold idea generation sessions routinely and have had success innovating new products, services and process improvements through their repeated use of basic techniques.

While brainstorming, these groups often find themselves coming up with the same ideas over and over again. A creative staleness or listlessness develops. After utilizing the fundamentals of idea generation, new perspectives, tools and energy are required. These teams need to be taken out of their idea generation comfort zone to push on to a higher echelon of accomplishment.

CREATIVE RUT IN ACTION: An IT group I worked with surrounding the challenge of how to improve their terrible customer service reputation wanted a totally different approach to the issue. This team had measures in place to monitor and improve customer interactions, had done training, and tried a variety of methods to make the situation better with no effect.

After spending a full day with them identifying problems, brainstorming and prototyping – working through an extensive process to tailor a solution to their problem and people – the group decided on a new and improved web site to address the issue. This web site was in no meaningful way any different from their current web site or any other web site in existence.

I asked the members of this team how many of them had thought about this "solution" before arriving at the workshop. Most said they did. I then asked them why we spent nine hours working to come up with a solution they had preordained.

This was a group that needed something to shock and change its thought processes out of a rut.

Breaking a team out of its creative rut to *improve the quality of ideas* often requires managers opening their minds to possibilities not previously considered. Creative ruts are often the result of a mindset which overly values "safe" or "easy" solutions, make an effort to take some risk with idea generation and pursue some unconventional ideas.

Scenario 3

The final response to my question comes from teams who are approaching an expert level with their brainstorming. They have the basics down cold and have become sharp and experienced at a variety of different idea generation tools and techniques. These teams make frequent ideation sessions a cornerstone of their operations and have experienced multiple successes because of their commitment to the practice of proven idea generation methods. Operating collaboratively to harness the collective brainpower of employees through the disciplined use of creativity tools, and the positive results experienced from working through that process time and again, has assured these people they can solve problems.

After taking the baby steps necessary to develop sound idea generation skills and gradually attempting and overcoming more and more challenging questions, they now want to stretch their legs and run to see how far they can push themselves creatively.

Me: "All right Jill, what results have you been getting from the brainstorming sessions you've held so far?"

Jill: "Michael, this is big. Our customer has really challenged us; challenged us to go way out. We've come up with a lot of ideas and a lot of good ones in the past, but they've largely been modifications or improvements on what we've done before. Our customer wants something new entirely, he wants to be wowed. We haven't gotten those results from what we've been doing."

When a team skilled and accomplished at idea generation faces a challenge so seemingly great or insurmountable that the methods it has used previously aren't powerful enough to overcome it, *breaking through to a new way of thinking* is required. Teams at this advanced stage of idea generation need to be moved, often forcibly, away from their current practices, even if those techniques have been successful. A willingness to accept risk and an openness to different approaches to problem solving are now required.

This approach may be necessary for groups wanting to creatively step beyond the immediate issues of the day and solutions presently thought possible. *Breaking through to a new way of thinking* proves effective when productivity is up and the specific business problem you're faced with seems hazy. The technique delivers when you're asked to develop a five-year plan or a customer comes to you asking for the moon. This strategy works for groups operating with the mindset that there has to be a better way.

Most of the teams I work with that want to adopt this approach aren't ready for it and still need much more practice with the basic and intermediary tools. The ability to successfully incorporate this technique rarely comes the first time I work with a team or even within the first six months; it develops only after a repeated practice of the basics which allows individuals to successfully take on more advanced methods.

Furthermore, *breaking through to a new way of thinking* requires a highly evolved manager or team leader willing to embrace a philosophy which may change the entire direction of the business or result in completely new products and services.

HELPFUL HINT: *Breaking through to a new way of thinking* is a technique especially suited to what are known as "Horizon 3" projects. Basically, Horizon 1 projects are those which will develop products, services or process improvements new to your company. Horizon 2 projects focus on those new to the industry. Horizon 3 projects concern concepts new to the world.

When your specific business problem involves finding solutions for the future, *breaking through to a new way of thinking* may be necessary. This advanced idea generation technique often demands individuals who search for unobvious connections between their industry and others; it requires greater and closer collaboration, deeper investigation, broader perspectives and more diverse opinions.

There are millions of unique business problems, hundreds of thousands of teams attempting to solve them, and only three idea generation obstacles preventing people from getting there. Identifying your brainstorming dilemma is the first step in solving those problems.

At this point in the creative process, tools are irrelevant. This stage centers on your team's brainstorming history and determining the reason for the roadblocks you're experiencing.

Following the countless seminars and speeches I've held on idea generation, everyone I talk to before and after wants to know where to start, how to start. You start by analyzing the results of your current idea generation sessions.

Teams who fail to undertake this step too often grab the first tool or book that comes along. Don't tie yourself to a technique that may be ill-suited to overcome the issue you're experiencing. Your selection of creativity tools should be based on the specific challenges and personality of your team, not what's "hot" in the industry or what you see other groups using.

You've put a culture of innovation in place and now you've identified your brainstorming deficiency. It's time for tools and the basics come first.

CHAPTER 7
Tools & Techniques for Increasing the Number of Ideas

The process of idea generation and innovation begins with small steps and a focus on the basics. Much of what I'm about to lay out in addressing your challenges with generating more ideas will seem rudimentary, it's meant to be. Consider this the walking necessary for your group to be able to run down the road.

The tools and strategies I'm going to provide you with are set up in order to be effective immediately and with no previous experience in idea generation. They also require no outside facilitation or cost. Despite the basic nature of the techniques detailed in this chapter, they must be mastered before moving on to more advanced strategies.

Focused Problem Statement

The first step in increasing the number of ideas is developing a *focused problem statement*. The old saying goes, "a problem well stated is a problem half solved." In order to effectively generate ideas, you have to define your problem, make it tangible, and give it context and parameters.

Think of it like this: if you walked up to a co-worker with a blank piece of paper and asked him to draw you a picture, he'd stare back at you with an equally blank expression.

"A picture of what," he asks.

"Anything," you reply.

His head cocks, his eyebrows furrow, he lets out an exacerbated sigh, "A picture of WHAT? Who's this for? What do you mean? A house? What should I draw it with? Where is this going?"

Giving someone a blank piece of paper and asking them to draw you a picture leads inevitably to confusion, frustration and lots of questions.

Our brains don't function that way. From infancy through adulthood, our minds have been trained to solve specific problems and answer questions, not create something out of nothing. That's why artists and inventors and creative people are special, they can design and imagine and make masterpieces where nothing previously existed. Ninety percent of us don't think that way.

Our brains need boundaries and defined problems to start working effectively. An unlimited, "everything is possible" approach to innovation contradicts with how the vast majority of our minds work and ends up being counterproductive. Ideas generated in this fashion are slow to materialize and widely scattered.

The more focused your challenge and the more specific the question you ask of your team, the more ideas you'll receive and the faster you'll receive them. If you say, "Draw me a picture," you'll get questions. If you say, "Draw me a picture of how we might redesign our office space," you'll get action and results.

A co-worker of mine at Cargill, Anne Rogers, had a great way of stating this "focus" issue as it relates to brainstorming using the tired business cliché, "thinking outside the box." She said, "We're not going to ask employees to think outside the box, we're going to provide them a new box to think in."

FOCUSED PROBLEM STATEMENT IN ACTION: One example of the importance of a *focused problem statement* from my personal experience surrounds the universal business challenge of cutting waste. A team leader asked me to evaluate and provide him some coaching on a brainstorming session he was about to hold. Sitting in the back of the room, I watched him write on a whiteboard the problem statement he wanted his group to work on: "How can we reduce waste?"

The room was quiet at first then an avalanche of ideas came forward.

"We need to install new conveyor belts so we don't waste as much product falling off the assembly lines."

"We can redesign our packaging to reduce waste there."

"If we had fewer meetings, we'd waste less time."

"We need to hire some part time employees because we're wasting money through excess overtime."

"If we started recycling, we would waste less paper."

This went on for 10 or 15 minutes before the manager realized his brainstorming session had no direction and he put a stop to it. Finally, he said, "What I was really thinking was that we are spending an obscene amount of money on energy costs and with those costs rising we need to reduce our energy waste; that's what I wanted to focus our brainstorming on."

His team members responded, "Oh, why didn't you say that to begin with?"

Remember the number one attribute of an innovative culture. Communication. A lack of communication doomed this brainstorming session to failure.

Before holding any idea generation meetings, communicate to your team the need for the meeting (soaring energy costs) and what you are going to ask of them (ideas on how reduce it). The positive impact this has on the upcoming session will be twofold: engagement and preparation.

By presenting a compelling need for the meeting you are making clear its necessity. Most employees are asked to go to enough meetings already; they want to know the importance of attending this one. Also, by soliciting ideas from your people about important business issues, you are demonstrating to them that you value their opinions and believe they have the ideas necessary to solve the problem. This show of respect will be rewarded with a fuller engagement on the employees' part.

Additionally, by tipping off your employees to the basic subject of the meeting, you will be mentally priming the pump of their brains so they arrive to the session with ideas, ready to contribute. In the "waste" example, employees were caught flat-footed by the problem and it took them time to get traction. Remember, when we ask our brain a question, it never stops working on the solution. It works harder some times than others, but it's always working. We can tap that awesome power by triggering employees' minds to the questions they'll be asked before actually asking them. Avoid springing questions on your people in meetings and allow them additional time to work on their solutions by informing them beforehand about what you're after.

A tremendous pet peeve of mine is showing up for a meeting and finding everyone turning to each other asking, "What are we here for?" You'd never call a meeting with your lawyer or accountant without informing them of the topic, why should employees be treated differently? People's time is precious and you want to maximize the time your group has together.

The teams that I've seen have the most success with generating more ideas are continually better prepared than other groups, and that preparation allows them to start solving problems the minute meetings begin.

In the meeting I described earlier communicating that a desire to "reduce energy waste" was going to be the focal point of the meeting would have pre-stimulated the thought processes of employees involved. This simple piece of communication would have provided the guidelines, boundaries and specific questions most people need to start solving problems.

As it happened, the group was caught off guard by the problem and since each team member worked in a different area of the business – office staff, production, human resources, management, and marketing – each of them viewed the word "waste" specific to their individual job responsibility. Office staff thought about paper waste, production staff thought about product waste, human resources thought about time and pay waste, management thought about resource waste, etc. It was a great idea to include people from throughout the company in the brainstorming session to assure different perspectives, but no one was working together. Ideas were isolated and not built upon. There was no collaboration, no singularity of purpose, everyone was moving in a different direction and the session was derailed.

Observing this meeting up close made it clear to me the importance of communication and focus to the idea generation process.

Let's explore this "waste" example and get specific about ways to make a "How can we reduce waste" idea generation session more effective.

Can vs. Might

The first thing I do when building a *focused problem statement* is changing "can" to "might." Idea generation is not about "can" or "can't," this is about "might." How "might" we do this?

At this stage in the process we want possibilities. When your group is challenged to generate more ideas an introduction of "can" limits ideas. The time for judging "can" or "can't" comes later. It's a simple word change and may seem small; however, it's a powerful linguistic trigger in our minds.

Our brains tend to get fixated on "can" and if someone wanted to present a seemingly wild idea, having "can" stuck in their mind might block them because they don't think the idea "can" be done. By using "might" we open minds and prevent members from filtering ideas which seem fantastic or outrageous. As much as we're trying to build focus into our idea generation sessions, once we come to that *focused problem statement* we want to encourage unorthodox ideas and what "might" be possible.

Oftentimes one employee's seemingly crazy idea sparks another team member to think about a different solution which creates a conversation and a momentum and suddenly that powerful group collaboration plows forward down a road you could never have imagined or explored by only thinking about safe ideas that "can" be done.

Imagine how many wonderful innovations the world would have been robbed of if in the idea generation stage the innovator was focused on "can" and "can't" instead of "might?" Besides, what "can" and "can't" be done changes all the time; what "can't" be done today, "can" be done tomorrow. As a facilitator, remember this as people start to critique and judge ideas. This step in the idea generation and innovation process is strictly about "might."

HELPFUL HINT: As you start this process and begin working with your group on focused problem statements, don't choose your biggest customer or top business obstacle initially. Start small, create successes, and allow your team to practice the methods I'm discussing before applying them to your greatest challenges.

You'll learn a lot about your team and its capabilities and the skills of your people by attempting this on a more limited scale. As you become more experienced and practiced and successful in idea generation, you can gradually work your way up to larger issues.

Key Words

Next, I break up the challenge statement to make it more specific. Look for key words. The most obvious in this example is "waste."

What types of waste does this business have: product waste, paper waste, energy waste, money waste, time waste, chemical waste?

Another key word would be "reduce."

In what ways might waste be reduced: by 10 tons, by 10,000 kilowatt hours, in half, by $50,000?

A third key word is "we."

Who might "we" be: the people at this table, the office staff, the employees at this location, full time employees, the entire company?

Three key words: energy, reduce and we.

How about adding a key word related to "time?"

When would you like this reduction of waste to take place: this quarter, this week, this year, daily?

Take those key words and create a column for each with the various possibilities listed below:

How	Might	We	Reduce	Waste	
		the people at this table	10 tons	product waste	
		the office staff	by 10,000 kilowatt hours	paper waste	
		the employees at this location	by half	energy waste	
		full-time employees	by $50,000	Money	
		the entire company		time waste	
				chemical waste	

Waste: product waste falling off the assembly line, paper waste, energy waste, money waste through excessive overtime pay, time waste, chemical waste.

Reduce: 10 tons, by 1,000,000 kilowatts, in half, by $50,000, individually.

We: the people at this table, the office staff, the employees at this location, full time employees, the entire branch, the entire company.

Time: daily, this week, this quarter, this year, monthly.

To create a *focused problem statement*, choose one word from each column such as: energy waste, by 1,000,000 kilowatts, the employees at this location, monthly. Rewrite your problem statement using those specifics: "how might the employees at this location reduce energy waste by 1,000,000 kilowatts monthly."

That's an effective problem statement. It's specific, it's actionable, and it still provides a great deal of flexibility to be creative with potential solutions while providing the focus necessary to drive a results oriented idea generation session.

HELPFUL HINT: Be careful not to make your problem statement too focused by providing a solution within it. For example, I've seen a focused problem statement written as, "How might the office staff reduce paper waste by recycling?"

The solution is recycling. If you want ideas for a recycling program for your office, adjust your problem statement to address that specifically such as "How might this office institute a recycling program in order to reduce waste."

A great benefit to this method is the number of potential

focused problem statements that can be generated out of each scenario.

How many *focused problem statements* could we develop from the above example? There are six types of waste, five specific reductions, six different "we" possibilities and five time break downs, that's 900 potential focused problem statements if we only used each one once!

Using this strategy to generate *focused problem statements* allows you to pick one – "how might the employees at this location reduce energy waste by 1,000,000 kilowatts monthly" – and if you start brainstorming and find none of the ideas generated seem capable of creating enough impact to make them worthwhile, you can easily select another – "how might paper waste be reduced in half by office staff daily" – and see what develops there. This allows you to experiment with multiple possibilities before devoting all of your time and efforts to any one problem statement.

Select a *focused problem statement* and start mining ideas around that challenge. See what develops and where it leads. Pick another one and mine it out for a few minutes. Explore various *focused problem statements* and see which ones most energize your group and where your team's ideas seemed to be most potentially productive; those are the solutions to pursue more fully.

HELPFUL HINT: I used to go through this process of developing a *focused problem statement* exclusively with the project sponsor and separate of the team. I figured it would save time and provide more control over the session. I've done an about-face on that philosophy and now see the incredible benefits to involving team members when developing a *focused problem statement*.

While you can simply present to your team its *focused problem statement*, "How might the employees at this location reduce energy waste by 1,000,000 kilowatts monthly," bringing members into the process of developing that statement has more advantages.

Presenting the *focused problem statement* without involving the team in its creation will make people wonder where it came from and why they are being asked to help solve it. I've found that by giving the team the overarching problem – "How might we reduce energy waste" – and then working together to shape that into the *focused problem statement* was well worth the additional time required.

Working together to make that overarching problem more specific made team members feel like they were a greater part of the process. It gave them additional ownership of the problem and further committed them to helping solve it.

Plus, the 10 minutes it takes to go from the overarching problem to the *focused problem statement* warms the group up to the additional work to come. It's like stretching before exercise.

That small change of including the team into the process of developing the *focused problem statement* made an immeasurable difference in the results I experienced in idea generation sessions. Put the experience of your people to use, reduce your own work load, and you know what, more than likely you'll come up with the exact same ideas.

Developing a *focused problem statement* is critical to increasing the number of ideas. In fact, if developing a *focused problem statement* is the only step you take in order to help your team generate more ideas, you will experience better results. If you commit to communicating to your team your overarching problem, encourage team members to help you craft that overarching problem into a *focused problem statement*, then take their ideas and provide timely and candid feedback on them, you'll be amazed at the stream of ideas that will flow in.

Brainwriting

Now that you've developed a *focused problem statement* you are ready to take the next step in the process of *increasing the number ideas* and the tool I recommend is *brainwriting*. *Brainwriting* works because it is simple, it can be done in person or virtually, and it doesn't require any facilitation skills or equipment.

What is brain-writing?

On a blank sheet of paper, write your *focused problem statement* at the top and then underneath it, fill the page with Post-it notes.

Hand out one of these sheets to each of the people at your meeting or on your team and give them roughly five minutes to write an idea for solving the *focused problem statement* in each sticky note – one idea per sticky note.

At the end of the allotted time, participants pass their sheet to the person at their right. Participants now read through the ideas already on the sheet and see if those ideas spark any new ones of their own. If they do, participants draw a line from the original idea to a Post-it containing the idea sparked by it. If the ideas on the sheet don't initiate any new ones, participants continue filling unfilled Post-its with their ideas.

Repeat this process until each participant gets their original sheet back, if a sheet gets full, provide an additional one.

I have used this tool hundreds of times with groups that are new to idea generation and innovation and have always found it to be successful in increasing the number of ideas. *Brainwriting's* ease of use and understanding makes it the best tool for this purpose.

It also allows all types of employees to contribute. I've mentioned the four different roles employees play in brainstorming, *brainwriting* harnesses the talents of each of them:

- The problem identifier will have played a major role in creating the *focused problem statement* through his vision of big-picture issues. Allowing this employee to help frame the session guarantees his engagement throughout.
- The idea person can go wild writing down ideas without monopolizing the session or having to wait his turn while others struggle to come up with their own. *Brainwriting* encourages volume and takes full advantage of this employee's reservoir of ideas.

- The editor can use the ideas other people have written to shape and modify them into ideas of his own without the pressure of having to create unique solutions. This member's skills are perfectly exercised as he's presented rough ideas to mold.

- The action person can use his special perspective of how things get done to further craft and modify existing ideas or approach solutions from a more practical point of view other members may lack.

The advantages of *brainwriting* don't stop there.

By providing everyone equal time to work on the problem, no employee dominates the session or disappears allowing individuals to contribute at their own pace. Ideas are written instead of verbalized so employees don't have to fear presenting before a group, a phobia which can utterly debilitate some employee's creativity. *Brainwriting* doesn't feature judgment or quotas or grades. People with numerous ideas are given the freedom to run while members with fewer are allowed to proceed more gradually.

HELPFUL HINT: What is the optimum group size for brainstorming? My experience has shown me that for groups working in this fashion, five to seven members are ideal.

In group dynamics, any time you have more than seven people, some members tend to get left out. If you have fewer than five, you risk not receiving enough ideas and lose the power that comes from each member being able to feed off the ideas of the others; groups this small lack the mental diversity necessary to experience a full spectrum of ideas.

If you have large groups – ten, 20, 30 people – split them into smaller groups and give each one a different and more focused challenge. By doing this you're able to multiply the power of the group by targeting different challenges instead of everyone duplicating the others' efforts. If you have 20 people working on the "waste" team, give one group "how might the employees at this location reduce energy waste by 1,000 kilowatts monthly," give another "how might paper waste be reduced in half by office staff daily" and give the third "how might this branch reduce money wasted through excessive overtime by $50,000 this year."

For groups inexperienced at idea generation *brainwriting* works because of its basic nature and it begins introducing employees to the ideation process.

Pool and Diversify

After the sheets have made it around to everyone in the group, you can begin organizing the ideas generated. Because all the ideas are written on Post-it notes, all those ideas can be stuck on a wall.

Immediately, you will see many duplicate ideas and find most ideas falling into a few general themes. Duplicate ideas are good; generally those are ideas worth pursuing since numerous people had them and they are typically the easiest to implement. Group the similar and duplicate ideas together on the wall and begin discussing their merits, potential, drawbacks, specifics and practicality. Build these ideas out and see which ones link and which need more clarification or focus.

Come to a consensus on the ideas you want to move forward with and then assign the responsibility of follow through. Take the ideas and get to work.

HELPFUL HINT: Consensus vs. Voting. Don't vote on ideas. Come to a consensus on ideas through communication and candor.

Voting causes hurt feelings and ideas to be excluded. When someone's idea gets voted down, you risk tuning that individual out from the rest of the process. If everyone agrees – or at least concedes – about which ideas should initially move forward, everyone remains engaged.

Voting encourages group think and rallying behind popular ideas and people.

Voting tends to favor ideas that seem most able to move forward over ideas best positioned to generate results.

Voting is easy. People raise their hands or write on a slip of paper and that ends the process and no one is forced to answer "why." Building a consensus demands ideas be defended and supported or critiqued and evaluated against other options.

Consensus building demands communication, candor and a reason. It allows one person the ability to convey the passion behind his preferred idea with the opportunity to sway the group instead of being steamrolled in a vote.

Consensus building is tough and yields far better results. The group as a whole needs to determine which ideas move forward to ensure those ideas has the highest degree of commitment.

We've all seen the movie "12 Angry Men" where one guy on a jury of 12 thought the defendant was innocent while the other 11 thought he was guilty and slowly, but surely, the one was able to sway the other 11 to his point of view – which turned out to be correct. The same moral applies here. Had the jury voted on guilt or innocence, the defendant would have been voted guilty immediately. The 11 who thought he was guilty wanted the process over, they wanted to go home; they weren't interested in depth or exploration. But since a jury must come to a consensus, the one man was allowed to express his concerns, open a dialogue, ask questions, force the others to confront the inconsistencies he saw, and over time, transfer his intuition to the rest.

Some people have great passion, but their ideas seem "out there" or "kooky" or hard to comprehend. Consensus provides that individual the opportunity to explain, communicate, and define his ideas for the others to better understand.

This doesn't mean that you allow one person to hijack the group and force it to stand in line behind an entrenched individual position. The team leader must determine when that starts taking place and how to best to handle it.

A sample agenda. If you're holding a session like this, here's the process you follow:

- communicate need and topic (before meeting starts)
- develop focused problem statement,

- hand out the brain-writing sheets,
- do the brain-writing,
- sort the ideas into themes.
- Discuss, add to, and build on ideas generated
- Consensus on top ideas to move forward or investigate further

Think of increasing the number of ideas as a continual process of diverging and converging. You begin with a broad problem statement then diverge by breaking it apart into key words.

Once it's broken apart, you converge to develop a *focused problem statement.*

When you arrive at your *focused problem statement,* you diverge again through *brainwriting* to generate as many ideas as possible.

Next, you converge by sorting the ideas into similar themes and deciding upon which themes to explore further.

After you've had discussions about the various ideas, converge again by coming to a consensus about which ideas will be carried forward and how.

HELPFUL HINT: Once you've determined the ideas you want to proceed with, you need to thank the people who were involved in the idea generation and ask them how they would like to be involved in the process going forward. Developing and selecting ideas is not the end of the road. Remember, innovation is the reward experienced after completion of the process, the end result. All you have now are ideas; you've yet to experience results.

What results you experience will be determined by your ability to manage the ideas generated. You'll need to find team members committed enough to the ideas to push them into realization.

Now the action people take over. Do you need to assign a project team to carry the ideas forward? If the project's scale is large, you may need to assign a management process, budget and timelines.

You need to regularly communicate back to the people involved in the idea generation about the status and progress of their ideas. You must keep these "ideators" in the loop or they will feel used and abandoned and lose their engagement and passion for the process.

I'm not a project management expert. My focus is generating ideas. How you manage the ideas you generate, however, and how they are followed through on is critical to experiencing results.

Use it or Lose it

I know what many of you are thinking: "Great! I'm on board! I can see the value in this and I can imagine it working for my team, but when should I use this?"

After teaching managers my strategies for increasing the number of ideas, I always finish the same way by giving them this *focused problem statement*: "How might my team incorporate these techniques into our regular practice?"

Just knowing this information doesn't generate more ideas or lead to innovation, it has to be practiced. If you don't find ways to use these techniques regularly, you will forget them and your team will never move beyond its infancy in idea generation. When, how, and how frequently you choose to practice these tools will be individual to you and your team and will be proportional to your success in generating more ideas.

Even if you don't have a pressing business or customer issue to apply this process to, you still need to practice. Lebron James doesn't practice his jump shot only when he has a game to prepare for; he is preparing all the time so he stays sharp and can then go to an even higher level of performance when his schedule demands it.

Lebron James practices the basics of his game constantly and so must you if you want to excel at idea generation. If you wait to use these strategies until you need them, you will be rusty and not well prepared to start working effectively.

If increasing the number of ideas matters to you, if it's important and something you're committed to, you'll find time for it somewhere in your week. And more than "finding" time for idea generation, "squeezing" it in, or working on it only when you feel you have time, you need to determine to "make" time for it.

This needs to become a part of what you do, not something special. Remember the values of a culture of innovation: to be innovative, you have to integrate it totally into your processes, not attempt it sporadically.

Think of how you might incorporate idea generation into your weekly meeting? How might you bring everyone together for lunch to introduce this priority? How might you take that final hour on Friday when everyone has already mentally checked out for the weekend to initiate this process as something energizing and provocative to finish the week?

To start with, try applying what you've learned here on basic issues like reducing waste or how to make meetings more effective. Pick a lighter topic such as how to remember your various computer login IDs or a fun subject like planning the Holiday Party. Begin thinking every day about how you might use these tools and techniques to solve your business' challenges regardless of what they might be.

View the use of these tools and strategies as a progression where the completion of each individual step will yield results and where their combination will be dynamic.

If you were only to develop a *focused problem statement* and properly communicate to your group the compelling reason to solve that problem, you will receive ideas and begin encouraging your team's imagination and creativity.

If all you did then was support your *focused problem statement* with regular communication to your team about where their ideas were in the process of solving that problem – had they been reviewed, what was your candid opinion of them, have they moved forward, which ideas are moving forward – you'd experience even greater results.

When you take the process all the way through its completion, when you facilitate a *brainwriting* session and then assign the necessary follow through and commit the resources required to complete the project, you will be an innovator. You will realize the value from those ideas.

You now have the blueprint and tools necessary to generate more ideas. As you and your team become more skilled with these strategies through consistent practice and the number of ideas you're receiving rises, you will work into a position where you can start introducing methods of *improving the quality of ideas*.

CHAPTER 8
Tools & Techniques for Improving the Quality of Ideas

I'm sure you're wondering why I don't jump straight to the *improving the quality of ideas* step and skip over generating more ideas. Aren't better ideas what we're all after?

You must walk before you can run. Idea generation is a progression. Individuals and teams have to practice and master the basics before advancing. I'm going to continually reinforce this critical message because of the temptation to bypass the simple fundamentals of idea generation in favor of more advanced tools and techniques.

The advanced methods I will detail use as their foundation the principles and exercises established earlier – communication, curiosity, focused problem statements, brain-writing, synthesizing ideas. If you try to apply the techniques I'm about to present for *improving the quality* of *ideas* without first becoming expert at the exercises for generating more ideas, you will fall short in your attempts at finding that next great innovation.

You've established a culture that values communication, curiosity, candor and commitment. Your team uses focused problem statements and brain-writing to generate more ideas. Your group has practiced the basics of idea generation, successes have been experienced, and employees are becoming polished at using those skills.

All of these positive developments are taking place and now you want more. You want breakthrough ideas. When you reach this point, you're ready to start introducing tools that will *help improve the quality of ideas.*

TOP 10 WAYS TO TELL IF YOUR IDEA GENERATION IS READY TO ADVANCE TO *IMPROVING THE QUALITY OF IDEAS*:

10. Your team has picked all the low hanging fruit

9. Ideas generated can best be described as "incremental" and "safe"

8. Ideas generated meet today's problems

7. Ideas generated are modifications of existing models or practices

6. Ideas generated represent the next logical step

5. Ideas generated can be instituted immediately with little effort

4. Ideas generated mainly confirm pre-existing solutions to problems

3. Your ideation has become routine and stale

2. The steaks have risen for your team and expectations are higher

1. You're falling back on tired devices like "Top 10" lists to stimulate people

Take pride in experiencing the results above – many businesses never get that far. The tools and techniques which result in *improving the quality of ideas* are designed to take you beyond those successes and help you develop the next generation, "wow" ideas that have the potential to change everything.

The best technique I've found to do this demands getting out of the office and seeing the world. I am challenging you to energize your brainstorming sessions by extending your reach for the information you're gathering. I want you to multiply and diversify the perspectives, behaviors and experiences you're considering. You need to broaden the scope on the viewfinder of your problems. You can do all of this through *observation*.

Observation has other names such as "human" or "user centered design" and the general philosophy remains consistent: using field observations to capture valuable information that can be fed into your creative process resulting in better ideas.

Observation centers on gathering information and pumping that information into your brainstorming sessions. *Observation* puts viewpoints, actions and data drawn directly from first hand experience at center stage. It's a *Gorillas in the Mist* approach where instead of reading books and theorizing about what "might be," you go into the field and watch and study and find out for sure what "is." *Observation* doesn't rely on speculation or assumption or stereotypes, it demands getting out of the office and seeing what actually takes place.

Basic brainstorming is limited because it only allows you to tap into the experiences, ideas and behaviors of the relatively few people on your team. Skillful observation allows a small team to gather as much, and often times more, information as hundreds of people could using introductory brainstorming techniques – and saves a fortune on catering. *Observation* mines large groups of people for all kinds of data and then feeds that wealth of intelligence into your idea generation.

This requires a significant change in how I want you to

approach idea generation. You will now not only be using the people on your team for ideas, you'll be utilizing huge groups of outsiders as well. Simple brainstorming effectively engages the employees on your team in the creative process; *observation* allows you to expand your available sphere of ideas to include the vast sea of people you don't work with. To be successful, *observation* demands going into the marketplace or workplace and gathering the insights, histories and conduct of customers, clients and the people who use your products, services or processes daily.

HELPFUL HINT: Observation vs. customer surveys. Observation goes beyond customer surveys and interviews. Actions speak louder than words and people are notorious for fudging the truth in their responses to questionnaires.

Ask the next 10 people you run into how many of them eat at McDonald's, shop at Wal-Mart or surf porn on the Internet. Due to a variety of reasons, the vast majority will say they don't do those things, but drive by a McDonald's or Wal-Mart parking lot and you'll notice it's always full and if you do any research on Internet usage you'll find pornography always a leading sector. Observed behaviors are far more reliable than surveys.

OBSERVATION IN ACTION: I've witnessed first hand the power of observation in generating better ideas numerous times, never more dramatically than with a group of leadership trainees I was teaching. I took this group through the entire innovation process from imagination to innovation and the challenge I gave them centered on how, with the proliferation of pay-at-the-pump, gas stations might drive more of their customers into the attached convenience stores where higher margins of profitability exist.

These trainees had no experience in the convenience store or gas station businesses and to fully understand the problem I knew we had to do more than sit around in a conference room speculating. To generate the best ideas possible we had to go out and watch people use gas stations and convenience stores.

In teams of five we fanned out all over town and spent the afternoon watching people pump gas and buy stuff in convenience stores. At the conclusion of the field work we regrouped to share our observations. Literally hundreds were discussed, but what struck everyone was that with the great majority of customers using pay-at-the-pump, people were standing besides their cars during fueling doing nothing.

No one checks their oil or tire pressure anymore. Few people wash their windows. Some would clean the trash out of their cars, but by and large, while their gas was pumping, customers stood idly watching. Team members realized these customers were a totally captive audience and soon focused their attention here. The new problem became how to reach out to these customers during the two or three minute fueling, grab their attention, then encourage them inside to the convenience store. The group noticed this gaping "customer connection opportunity" by moving out of the office and *observing*, an opportunity we likely would have missed talking around a table.

This example demonstrates the power of *observation*.

Another tremendous benefit of *observation* comes through the greater understanding team members have of the challenge they're asked to confront after having observed the processes and behaviors related to that issue. When people *observe*, they gain knowledge.

If I'd asked my leadership group at the beginning of the day to talk to me for five minutes about gas stations, gas pumps, convenience stores and the experience of fueling a car, they would have struggled to fill 60-seconds. Individuals could have told me their personal stories about pumping gas, but after spending two hours at four different gas stations around town the members had gathered statistics about who pumped gas, how women pumped gas differently from men, what types of cars customers drove, and these statistics were as up-to-date as possible having been gathered that day. The team knew how long it took to pump gas, which customers went inside the convenience store, what those people typically bought, how people paid for gas and how much gas they were buying.

Team members took their *observation* a step further by talking to the employees about the customers who came inside the store. What they bought, how much time did they spend inside the store, how did they pay, and what questions did they ask. They talked to customers about what they liked or disliked about the gas station, how the experience could be improved, and what they would be interested in buying in the convenience store.

Following the *observation*, where novices once sat for brainstorming, a room full of experts now appeared.

We ended up spending three hours after the observation talking about pumping gas. We filled 45-feet of wall space with data. Some team members spent 30-minutes themselves presenting. If I'd tried to do any of that before the observation, the session would have flopped. Remember, this group had zero background in the gas station or convenience store business; imagine the information and solutions that could have been gathered if they had been observing something they were already expert at and experienced in.

HELPFUL HINT: Now you bring back the principles of focused problem statements and brainwriting. You've gathered the outside information and it's been presented and shared with the entire team. Start working it through the idea generation process.

Synthesize the information; bucket the key observations, trends and customer profiles and give them names. Focus on the one or two areas which seem to have the greatest potential for results.

With the "convenience store" team it was the dead period during fueling and how to hook those customers and get them into the store. Develop a focused problem statement based on that observation – "how might we increase in-store sales through connecting with customers during the fueling lag time" – and start your brainstorming or brainwriting. Be sure to keep all the other information you've gathered so you can mine it later if the focused problem statement you choose initially doesn't gather momentum or if you decide to attack the challenge from other angles.

By the conclusion of my time with the leadership team we had developed a prototype for a new gas pump which had a TV screen where commercials would run advertising specials on products available in the convenience store enticing more people inside. To better capture that customers' attention, the monitor would also show news, weather and traffic updates.

We invited an owner of one of the gas stations we visited into our conference room to present him the prototype and get his feedback. Reviewing our observations, information gathered, and ideas generated, he couldn't believe we didn't work in the convenience store and gas station business. He was amazed at the insights we had gained about his business and customers, as outsiders, in one afternoon.

After thanking us for the ideas, he left saying he'd run the info past his corporate bosses. Now I'm not taking credit for this, but two years later I returned to his station and found it had fully interactive screens at the pumps. These monitors featured entertainment content as well as advertisements about products available in the store filling that dead time customers were experiencing. Ideas that good do not come from meeting rooms with a, "how do we get people to go inside," challenge statement on a whiteboard. Those ideas are inspired by leaving the office and *observing.*

HELPFUL HINT: Encourage participants to gather artifacts during field research. This powerful technique makes *observation* even more effective. When individuals share pictures, diagrams, fliers, products or any other tangible materials that strike them as impactful or useful in "ideation" sessions, those sessions become that much more valuable and potentially able to generate results.

Observation doesn't require a lot of time, it's simple to explain and perform, there's no cost associated with it, and most importantly, it works! As a manager, you need to challenge your people to embrace this advanced technique and create opportunities to use it.

Push your team out of the office. Encourage individuals to explain what they're observing and why it's taking place. Engage your curiosity by asking team members why customers or employees are acting the way they are, or why they're not acting how you'd like them to. Challenge people to think about how seemingly minor details could be important.

If you're looking for a way to introduce *observation* to your team, develop a focused problem statement and brainstorm opportunities for observation such as "where might this team be able to use *observation* in the next month to solve a specific business challenge?"

While *observation* represents only one of the many techniques available to help teams *improve the quality of ideas*, its versatility contributes to making it the best method for doing so. *Observation* can be effectively applied in a variety of ways.

I've demonstrated the power of *observation* when directed outwardly in the marketplace; its power works as well when applied internally by observing the processes, people and behaviors at your workplace with the same goal in mind: gathering information to fuel idea generation.

Obvious problems or solutions regularly present themselves immediately once individuals take the time to push away from their desk and look around. A story, now grown more into legend, describes an engineering intern touring a production facility with a 15-year employee who'd walked that floor thousands of times. The kid started looking around and then started asking questions: where does this go, why is this here, what does that do, whose job is this, etc.

One of his questions stumped the guide which led to further investigation that resulted in one machine being eliminated, resulting in a $500,000 yearly energy savings.

Employees at that location had become desensitized to their

surroundings. They had fallen into a routine which had them drifting through work, content to focus only on their individual responsibility. These were good employees, bright employees who hadn't been challenged to question the status quo or use their expertise and *observation* skills to assist the business. The result of this was a glaring inefficiency hiding for years in plain sight.

Process optimization and the elimination of all kinds of waste are the routine result of internal *observation*. This internal *observation* goes hand-in-hand with one of the core values of an innovative culture: curiosity. Rewarding employee curiosity and encouraging observation opens a world of potential enhancements.

Not only can new employees using *observation* spot internal opportunities for improvements, long time employees pushed out of their comfort zones can yield even greater results. A wonderful story was shared with me about internal *observation* and its use at Toyota.

OBSERVATION IN ACTION: When U.S. and Japanese firms first started collaborating on processes and techniques, a Japanese plant manager was put in place at a U.S. facility. He led one of the location's existing supervisors through an unusual – and highly effective – *observation* exercise.

The plant manager drew a circle in chalk on the production room floor and told the supervisor to stand inside it for an hour! The plant manager gave the supervisor some paper, a pen, and then left.

For the first 10 minutes, the supervisor was fuming! He threatened to quit, he shouted about how this was B.S., how he couldn't be treated this way, and how he didn't have to put up with this garbage! He eventually calmed down and with nothing else to do, started looking around.

He noticed people, equipment and the rhythm of the work. After watching for a few more minutes he began jotting notes. He started with small issues like cleanliness and idle employees. Soon he was recognizing production line choke points, poor ergonomics and waste of every kind.

After 30 minutes he couldn't write fast enough with everything he was observing.

The man saw lighting problems, inattentive employees, safety concerns and wide-ranging potential operation enhancements. This sparked him to think about new product ideas and a better design for the assembly line. When the Japanese plant manager returned after an hour, the American supervisor asked for more paper and another hour in the circle.

I've seen this progression take place with groups I've lead through internal *observation*. Team members sent on these exercises always start thinking, "What are you going to teach me; I've been doing this for years." That initial resistance gradually gives way to some passive observation and thoughts of, "hmm, that's interesting."

The progression then kicks into high gear. One observation leads to another and in rapid succession closer scrutiny of behaviors and processes has the participant thinking, "Wow, I can't believe I've missed that" or "I never thought about that before!"

The opening of this previously unseen world stimulates a tremendous excitement to discuss and share their new ideas and perspectives. You will experience this progression with your team members once you get out where the action is.

When initiating internal *observation*, be sure to communicate to employees your purpose in order to avoid needless suspicion and rumor. As *observation* continues, you'll find employees beginning to share their own observations and experiences, both internally and externally. This will generate even more information. All that data will create an incredibly powerful engine to drive your brainstorming sessions far beyond anything you've previously experienced.

I have one last challenge for you: be an active observer yourself. Don't miss opportunities to watch people and processes and use those observations to fuel idea generation. Make this a part of how you walk through the world. *Observation*, like all the other skills I'm presenting, requires practice to master. What makes *observation* different is that there are chances to practice it everywhere.

Having worked for years on my observation skills, everywhere I go I notice traffic flows, layouts, waste, choke-points and any number of a dozen other processes and behaviors. I've become a dreadful companion to go shopping with because these are the things I notice and comment on in stores. I'm constantly analyzing floor designs, why products are placed where they are, what inefficiencies exist. I look at products, packaging, signs, sales, employee uniforms and activities. I talk regularly to employees about how the store operates and why things are done the way they are.

I've done so much observation I can't turn it off and I challenge you to do the same. You might become a pain to browse with at Macy's, but you will be a vastly better idea generator and innovator. I want you to start looking at the world through the lens of potential innovation. Lead the *observation* efforts of your team by championing them yourself. Potential solutions to your business challenges are everywhere if you'll make the effort to observe them.

CHAPTER 9
Tools & Techniques to Break Through to a New Way of Thinking

In 1982 when the EPCOT theme park opened at Walt Disney World in Orlando, Florida, a reporter on the scene commented to Roy Disney, brother of the late Walt Disney, "Isn't it a shame Walt isn't here to see this?" Roy responded to the reporter without hesitation, "Walt saw this 30 years ago, that's why we're standing here today."

After learning to generate more ideas and then better ideas, the next frontier of idea generation is channeling your inner Walt Disney and *breaking through to a new way of thinking*. You do this by instituting a *futures mindset*.

Decades before it opened Walt Disney imagined a planned community of the future to be located in what was then an uninhabitable swamp in The Middle of Nowhere, Florida. It was an audacious idea that drew ridicule at the time, but Disney was operating with a *futures mindset* and this level of thinking demands a degree of boldness and risk.

When we go through basic brainstorming we're trying to address immediate needs, put out fires, grease the squeaky wheel and solve the problems of today. While that is an important function of idea generation, when you're after innovations that can amaze customers, catapult you into the future and separate yourself from the competition, you need to break through to a new way of thinking.

This challenge necessitates moving your creative process beyond merely solving problems to a place where you begin anticipating the needs of the future, needs people don't even realize they have or will have.

In the early 1960's, housewives weren't saying, "I wish I had an oven the size of a couple toasters which could heat my food in seconds and never get hot inside." Customers weren't demanding the microwave. No one then was thinking about how the ability to cook Salisbury steak in 90-seconds could allow millions of bachelors to live exclusively off frozen food; fortunately, an accident in a laboratory lead to a spark of imagination which fed creativity resulting in a prototype that ended up becoming an innovation that changed the way America eats. The *futures mindset* seeks out the next microwave by visualizing the future and innovating solutions to unmet needs.

Most people think the future just somehow happens. Remember Richard Branson? When he was a kid, he thought someone would eventually come along and develop commercial space travel and all he had to do was wait for it. He waited and waited and it didn't happen, he had to make it happen.

The future doesn't just happen, people innovate it when they move from a focus of solving the problems of today to a consideration of what their business and industry will look like five to 10 years or more from now.

HELPFUL HINT: I can hear you saying, "That's a big job:

predicting the future and innovating solutions to needs people don't even know they have!"

It is challenging there's no doubt about that. This idea generation obstacle, however, like all the others we've discussed, has a starting place, a progression, and a set of basic techniques which, when broken down into steps, makes the possibility much more manageable.

For starters, if you get to this point, congratulations! When you find your culture of innovation firmly established and your people so skilled and sharp with their basic brainstorming, brainwriting and observation that all of your immediate business challenges are being met and the only area remaining for you to explore becomes the future, treat yourself to the best restaurant in town for a job well done. Once you've drilled the basics, practiced them repeatedly, worked numerous ideas all the way from imagination through innovation and believe your team's full potential can now only be met by entirely changing the way it thinks about problems, you are an innovator and I am proud of you.

For achieving this, your reward is the tremendous challenge and opportunity of determining the future. I've used the "crawl before you walk" analogy before – brainstorming is crawling, brain-writing is walking, observation is running, changing the way your employees think about problems through an incorporation of the futures mindset is competing in the Olympic decathlon. While an advanced technique, if you've built a solid foundation of innovation with your employees you can do this and innovating for the future has the potential to be one of the most exciting initiatives your team can undertake.

The chief obstacle to incorporating a *futures mindset* is that it doesn't come naturally. In order to change the way your employees think about problems, you have to reprogram their minds. The establishment of a *futures mindset* requires employees to think counter to the way they've been trained to think all of their lives.

Ninety-nine percent of our problem solving ability works towards issues and problems of the day: what to wear to work, prepare for meeting with Jennifer at 10:30, forms to fill out, e-mails to respond to, where to go for lunch, have to pick up dry cleaning at five, what's the best way to get there? People are trained to be problem solvers. We have been conditioned to handle today's pressing issues, go to sleep, wake up, and do it all over again.

Pulling employees out of that mindset and placing them into one that envisions the world of the future is formidable. Fortunately, resources and exercises exist to help accomplish this and the potential benefits are staggering.

The need for a teachable method to transition employees into a *futures mindset* was a project I had wanted to tackle for years. I realized it couldn't wait any longer after a series of more and more frustrating idea generation sessions I was facilitating with teams in the food industry.

Coming up with ideas wasn't the problem for these groups, their problem was being so stuck in the mindset of solving the challenges of the day that they couldn't envision any solutions that were new, unique or breakthrough. Unconsciously, these teams had built huge walls around their idea generation and hemmed in their potential by exclusively viewing their challenges through today's eyes.

One team trying to sell more product became fixated on the idea of using the endorsement of a celebrity chef, another wanted to take its brand into low-carbohydrate offerings, a third centered its solutions around the ability to order products on-line and have them delivered to customers at home. These were good ideas and they were five years too late. I was working with these groups in the mid-2000's and by that time the celebrity chef fad along with the low-carb craze and a rush to put everything on-line were played out. These ideas were tantamount to developing a better 8-track tape player in 1980. It was time to move on.

Trends in the food industry move fast and these groups had already missed out on the leading edge of those movements. Trying to catch up would put them in on the back end where results are small, if experienced at all.

I knew simply imploring these employees to think differently would never transition them to a place where they could begin imagining the future. That change requires a shift in mindset too dramatic to go through without any specific guidance or coaching. What was necessary were a set of tools to bridge the gap between how these people were thinking, how most people think, and the *futures mindset* necessary to start developing the breakthrough ideas companies are demanding.

To assist the transition I set about creating progressive exercises that could help lead any group of people from a focus on the present into a mindset of inventing for the future and solving unmet needs.

Whenever I begin introducing a team to the *futures mindset* I always start with this question: how many people here have the ability to predict the future? No one initially raises their hand; I do.

I keep my hand up without saying anything else, accepting the strange looks and allowing the class to think more about the question. I see the gears in their minds working. Team members' thought processes start with, "I wish I could; I'd put my 401K on a 10-team parlay in Vegas and leave this seminar for Bermuda."

Gradually, they remember they're in an innovation class, we're talking about the future and they know I have no supernatural powers that allow me to see tomorrow. They begin to view the future, as we're discussing it, as something they have control over. Eventually, another hand goes up, then another and another. By the time every hand in the room is raised, the team is united about what it will be working toward: predicting the future by creating it. Through innovation, predicting the future becomes a matter of choice, calculated risk-taking, and effort.

Once a group understands and believes it has the ability to shape the future I always pull an example relative to the business I'm working with that shows how a team in this field should have been able to predict the future and the tremendous benefit it could have reaped from doing so. There are thousands of examples of this in literally every sector and finding one that applies to your team will be easy.

- How long were customers and experts telling American automakers to improve their product quality and transition to smaller, more fuel efficient models with no action from Detroit? After decades of warnings and a dramatic loss of market share to foreign competitors, the bottom finally dropped out on the Big Three American automakers in the late 2000's with massive plant closings and layoffs, the need for government bailout, and bankruptcy for General Motors and Chrysler.
- It's well documented that Folgers saw Starbucks coming and laughed at the idea that anyone was going to spend $3 for a cup of coffee. Instead of branching out, Folgers stayed

in the commodity business buying and selling bulk coffee and has been left in the dust by Starbucks as a purveyor of "venti iced-mocha latte with whip and an extra shot."

- Netflix was founded in 1997, went public in 2002, but it wasn't until 2004 that Blockbuster entered the on-line movie rental marketplace. Blockbuster has been eclipsed by Netflix as the nation's top video rental company and according to a 2009 article on moneymorning.com, "Blockbuster's operating income at the end of its second quarter in 2004 was $105.3 million. That was just before Netflix entered mainstream consumer consciousness. Blockbuster's operating income at the end of its second quarter this year was a loss of $1.5 million."

- In 2006 the animal feed business was going through a terrible slump because widespread government sponsored ethanol subsidies had dramatically raised the price of corn, the main ingredient in animal feed. Where previously corn cost $2 a bushel, its price rapidly doubled leaving animal nutrition companies struggling to meet demands and turn a profit. Who could have ever predicted the price of corn doubling in a year because of ethanol subsidies? A book titled "2025" did that exact thing. The book was published in 1998. That book and that prediction have drawn more than a few gasps from animal feed teams I have worked with on the problem of how to survive a marketplace where the price of corn has skyrocketed.

The future almost never appears as a lightning bolt out of a clear blue sky, much more typically it will hint at its arrival for years.

So how can this be used? How can you use trends, research

and your expectations of what the future of your industry will look like to innovate for the needs of tomorrow?

I suggest using the following prediction to introduce you and your team to this method of idea generation; consider it a warm-up exercise. Start your team's utilization of the *futures mindset* by approaching the problem of population growth. I have employed this example numerous times with groups in widely varied industries and always find it successful.

"FUTURES MINSET" IN ACTION – Global census takers agree that by 2050 the world's population will hit nine billion. It was only in 2008 that the planet's population hit six billion. That means over the next 40 years our population is expected to increase again by half.

To adequately feed all those people, over the next 40 years we'll have to create as much food as has been created in all of human history. That calculation stuns readers and is a belief widely held by experts – experts paid and trained to predict the future. Let your team absorb that information then ask these questions:

1. How might that change impact you personally over the next 40 years?
2. How might it impact your business?
3. What is it that your key customers might need as a result of this?
4. What might your business or company look like in 2050 as a result?
5. What products or services might you need to have to maximize profits during this time?
6. When do you feel you should start working on the products or services that can take advantage of this situation?

Each one of those questions leads to a mini brainstorming session within the group where you spend 20 or 30 minutes discussing. Approach the questions in order as they are progressive and systematically move an individual's mindset through a natural process which ultimately allows them to tackle what can be vast and nebulous challenges.

Question five, "What products or services would you need to have to maximize profits during this time?" will help your business and may be what you're most interested in, but if you start your team members brainstorming around that question immediately without leading them up to it by asking the preceding questions, most likely they'll find the challenge too daunting and idea generation will be stunted.

Questions one through four serve as a series of stepping stones leading your team to question five. When we're posed with a situation, we instinctually think how that information will impact us – question one. Our brains then move to our next sphere of influence, our jobs (question two), then to our customers (question three) and eventually to the world at large (questions four and five). Question six completes the series bringing the team back into the present by demanding action.

Questions one through five rely on imagination and creativity; question six begins the process of innovation. As you move through these steps watch as the ideas generated by your team branch out to include different business models and fantastically imaginative products and services. Notice the energy created by taking on the future and how team members' thought processes begin to evolve from an exclusive focus on the present to a consideration of tomorrow.

The next step in applying your team's burgeoning *futures mind-set* requires finding an issue and future scenario specific to your business to start working on. This can be another opportunity for your team to practice developing focused problem statements and brainstorm. "What future trends or predictions might this team start focusing on for our business to take advantage of?"

If you already have trends, scenarios or predictions in mind, great, if not, there's no need to struggle in finding them. Information and predictions about the future of your sector are everywhere from trade publications, books, on-line sources and your own intuition. To augment what you find on your own, there exists an organization called the World Future Society whose members spend their time analyzing data and conducting research intended to predict the future.

The World Future Society (www.wfs.org) publishes a book each year entitled *The State of the Future* which can serve as a tremendous resource for anyone trying to find thoughtful, detailed, exhaustively researched predictions for tomorrow and beyond. *The State of the Future* includes forecasts for nearly every industry and aspect of life from travel, communications and education to science, technology and the environment. In the interest of full disclosure, I am a member of the World Future Society, but my connection to them in no way influences my support of its work, its accuracy, or my belief in its ability to assist your idea generation.

The State of the Future and the other publication I highly recommend to spur your *futures mindset*, the World Future Society's annual "Outlook Report" which features its most thought-provoking forecasts for the year, aren't vague, fortune teller nonsense. These predictions are the best estimates from the top experts about how our world will change five, ten, fifty years and more down the road. You can't trust every statistic or prediction as absolute, but you can certainly gather enough information and use your own experience and common sense to determine the future trends your industry and what will likely transform it in the coming years.

After choosing a scenario or prediction specific to your industry and communicating your interest in undertaking this exercise, ask team members the same questions from the global population example above; those same questions are used to start all future-focused brainstorming sessions. At this point, you follow the progressive idea generation steps I have previously established:

1. Develop a focused problem statement
2. Perform brain-writing
3. Sort the ideas into themes
4. Mine those ideas down in further detail
5. Determine which ideas have the most promise or create the most energy among the group
6. Come to a consensus about which of those ideas to pursue
7. Task follow-through

Don't be Chairman of the Bored

As I began developing exercises to encourage a *futures mindset,* I started thinking about the people who are happy and unhappy in their jobs. The more thought and observation I gave the issue, the more clear it became to me what common bond the unsatisfied employees shared: boredom.

Employees stuck in a rut, performing the same routine daily, bound to an ordinary or mundane work experience are rarely engaged in their work and functioning at maximum capacity.

Conversely, those who achieve and stand out have goals that push them to excel. Innovation works the same. If all your efforts are targeted at handling daily problems and continually working through similar challenges and exercises, you and your team will become bored.

Groups incorporating a *futures mindset* into their brainstorming do concern themselves with the present while also allowing themselves to reach out and work on a vision for what the future they want looks like. This keeps the process fresh and evolving and stimulates the minds of employees maintaining their engagement and productivity.

Thinking for the future and handling the problems of today need not be an "either/or" decision, both can be achieved simultaneously. A perfect example of this balance in practice takes place at Google where all employees are allocated 20% of their regular work time to focus on new projects that interest them. That's a full day each week.

Google does not treat thinking about tomorrow as a luxury or frivolity; it takes place every day as a part of its regular operations. Many of Google's most recent and popular innovations – Gmail, Google News, Orkut and AdSense – originated from these independent endeavors.

During a 2006 speech at Stanford University, Marissa Mayer, Google's Vice President of Search Products and User Experience, stated that her analysis showed 50% of the company's new product launches originated from this 20% "innovation time off." That powerful return on investment demonstrates how the *futures mindset* can deliver concrete, bottom-line results.

As important as those innovations are to Google's bottom line, the "license to pursue dreams" as Mayer calls it, has an additional benefit at Google and it comes in the area of employee engagement which I've stressed previously.

"The key is not 20% of your time," said Mayer, "It's that engineers and product developers realize that the company trusts them and wants them to be creative and explore what they want to explore and it is that license that fuels a tremendous amount of creativity and innovation."

Within the technology field, Google doesn't offer employees the highest pay. With that being the case, how come Google remains one of the most desired companies to work for? The positive, supportive, engaging work environment at Google which doesn't only allow, but demands people to follow their individual passions, far surpasses any salary shortcomings in workers' minds.

I'm not saying 20% is the magic number when it comes to time which should be spent imagining the future (at 3M it's 15%); individual leaders and teams can determine that. I am saying that making sure an eye stays continually focused on tomorrow and that resources are devoted to making sure your team gets there will pay huge dividends.

The Feather, the Brick or the Truck

Opportunities to see the future and act before its arrival show up constantly and sooner or later you will have to deal with it. When the future presents itself, will you respond to the feather, the brick or the truck?

The future comes on by degrees with the feather being that subtle tickle which gets your attention, often being ignored as you focus on more pressing and immediate matters. You know in the back of your mind that the tickle will eventually need to be reckoned with and because you're so caught up in the issues of the day, you still neglect it.

The future arrives inevitably and if you have failed to act on the tickle, it will whack you on the head like a brick. At this point, you are certain of your need to address future concerns, however many of us simply pick ourselves up, dust ourselves off, and press forward on our normal course, too busy to take the time to look beyond today's concerns.

You've been given two warnings and haven't yet had to pay dearly. You will when your refusal to anticipate and prepare for the future manifests itself as a truck running you over leaving you splattered in the street and breathing exhaust while it barrels down a road you ignored with your competitors in the cab. Now you have no choice, but to respond to the future and find yourself flat on your back, often hopelessly unprepared to even catch up, let alone pass, your future-focused competition.

You may laugh at this analogy, but how many of you have ignored minor health problems, claiming to be too busy to have them checked out or hoping they'd go away, only to see them become much bigger problems because they weren't treated at first symptom?

The future works the same way: it's coming and it's going to be big. You choose which point you want to start preparing for and addressing it, the feather, the brick or the truck?

The sports television network ESPN has consistently acted on the feather routinely pacing the sports media world with innovative new content and delivery platforms. For more than 25 years, it has changed and dictated how fans consume sports and left a trail of would-be competitors in its future-focused wake.

Sony waited for the truck which was digital music and the

i-Pod. Sony's Walkman owned portable music for years; now that company and brand are virtually invisible in the portable music marketplace because of a refusal to work on the innovations of tomorrow, today.

Utilizing a *futures mindset* conditions you away from a singular obsession with the moment and trains you to notice those signs of the future that appear with a small tickle, the feather, and capitalize on them. In hindsight, we can easily say a business or individual should have acted on a hint of some future development because we're all risky, willing and bold when it comes to events which have passed. Recognizing those signals when they first arise demands thinking in ways most of us are unaccustomed to. That evolution requires *breaking through to a new way of thinking* by starting to put a focus beyond today.

Your Legacy

Great power can be found in an ability to see the future. You will also find risk. You make the decision of which trends and predictions to pursue and take a chance on. The reward for taking this risk can become your legacy. You have the ability to bring the future to people by adopting these techniques and when you do, your efforts will always be remembered.

Embrace the future, its potential, and your ability to shape it.

Think big, so big that it drives you continually. Avoid a preoccupation with how long a project or new idea may take to be completed.

I want to share with you a quote from biologist Wes Jackson, "If your life's work can be accomplished in your lifetime you're not thinking big enough."

Walt Disney never saw Epcot, John F. Kennedy never saw a man walk on the moon, and both achievements remain their legacy because they had the courage to imagine them. That courage was accompanied by a wisdom which allowed them to envision needs for the future most others couldn't see and the determination to put their ideas on a track to completion, no matter how long it took. *Breaking through to a new way of thinking*, instituting a *futures mindset*, considering the world of tomorrow and taking action to make it happen, use these techniques to leave your mark on the world.

PART IV

There's a Gleam

CHAPTER 10
What's Old is New Again

Innovation requires more than cultures, tools, strategies, and ideas. People determine its ultimate success or failure. People like you, people who either choose to derail innovation out of their fear of change, or those who promote it, lead it, manage it, champion it and make it happen.

Culture and tools can't do anything without the industry and leadership of individuals who take on the responsibility of putting them into practice. In every organization, innovation needs someone to step forward and light the fuse; that contribution can be made by any team member regardless of their place in the hierarchy.

A great misconception about innovation states that its introduction must come from upper-management. Innovation's flexibility and scalability allows it to be implemented at any level of an organization, including the individual level. You don't need a key to the executive washroom to begin applying the lessons of this book.

Every group I talk to about innovation invariably asks me what the key leadership principles necessary to become successful at innovation are. My answer: all of them.

Don't let that scare you. You don't need to posses every leadership skill known to man; you only need to understand how the leadership skills you already posses apply to innovation. There are no leadership skills specific or unique to innovation separate from the leadership skills required in any other walk of life. This philosophy is exclusive to my approach to the subject. All the standard, long-held, and widely-accepted leadership principles that the business world agrees on apply perfectly to innovation.

Think of it like this: are there traits that any leader has that shouldn't be shared by leaders of innovation? Leaders are required to have vision, be strong communicators, passionate, organized and intelligent. They're asked to have boldness, an ability to seize opportunities and an innate knack for motivating others among many other abilities.

Are any of those skills unnecessary for a leader of innovation? Does an innovator not need to be organized or passionate? Are vision and boldness not required of a leader of innovation? Of course not. No leadership trait generally applicable to the wider business environment cannot also be applied to innovation, the important element becomes understanding how those traits apply.

To be a leader of innovation you don't have to learn anything new or different or change what you already believe about leadership, you only have to comprehend how what you already know applies to innovation. I will show you how the implementation of any and every widely accepted philosophy of leadership will positively impact your innovation efforts.

Each of the traits I'll present is important to innovation, but none more than any other. You decide for yourself which ones you'd most like to focus on, or simply stick with the leadership characteristics your team already values and begin viewing them through the prism of innovation. You can't go wrong here. Whichever traits you choose or currently practice will assist your team's innovation efforts once you understand how they apply.

There are hundreds of different leadership traits and principles, instead of detailing how each can foster greater innovation, I'll address those most often referenced and then you can determine how your individual interpretation of leadership works with innovation. By the end of this chapter I hope you will see how the leadership traits you already posses only make you that much more prepared to be a leader of innovation.

Our examination of the links between general leadership skills and leadership in innovation begins with the most common characteristics of effective leaders mentioned in virtually all of the thought on the subject. You will find these attributes instantly recognizable as they form the foundation of virtually every book you read or seminar you attend on leadership and include, in one fashion or another:

STRONG COMMUNICATOR
RISK TAKING
VALUE DIVERSITY
FOCUSED
STRATEGIC THINKING
ABILITY TO WORK COLLABORATIVELY
and BUILD PARTNERSHIPS

You've read many of these words and phrases previously in this book so I won't belabor the connections; I do want to make clear how they each apply to innovation.

• STRONG COMMUNICATOR: Particularly in establishing an innovative culture and throughout the entire process of innovation, you must have an ability to effectively communicate your ideas. The innovation results you experience will be determined by how well you share your passion for innovation, explain its potential rewards, and deliver candid feedback during the brainstorming process.

- RISK TAKING: Innovation requires change and change involves risk. Innovation breaks away from the status quo and moves organizations and people out of their comfort zones. Leaders able to embrace and manage this risk are better positioned to adapt and benefit from the inevitable changes innovation brings and guide their teams through these sometimes choppy waters.
- VALUE DIVERSITY: Whether building teams composed of diverse employees or encouraging brainstorming sessions that feature a diversity of thought, innovation demands a widely varied set of people and viewpoints to maximize its potential.
- FOCUSED: Innovation offers a world of possibilities, so many in fact that if goals aren't well-defined and the process harnessed, the great expanse of its potential can swamp teams. Understanding that innovation's greatest potential will be experienced when applied to specific challenges with clear boundaries often separate the innovation contenders from the pretenders. The value of this trait can be found by looking no further than "focused problem statements."
- STRATEGIC THINKING: The strategic leader appraises customer needs and market trends, analyzes the capabilities and limitations of teams, predicts opportunities and when to capitalize on them in order to steer innovation towards

the opportunity for best results.

- ABILITY TO WORK COLLABORATIVELY and BUILD STRONG PARTNERSHIPS: Innovating features a number of distinct stages from imagination and creativity to the development of prototypes, project management and oftentimes marketing. Coordinating these steps and the people required to undertake them demands collaboration as well as an ability to bring team members with varied skills, job descriptions and interests together.

The above are the most general, over-arching, common leadership skills discussed across all businesses. Each and every one of them has a direct connection to innovation.

Why don't we see if the same holds true with a more individual philosophy of leadership? Longtime General Electric Chairman and CEO Jack Welch, widely regarded as one of the most influential and successful business leaders over the last half century, defined four unique attributes of effective leaders:

ENERGETIC
ENERGIZES OTHER PEOPLE
HAS AN EDGE
EXECUTES

Welch didn't construct his leadership principles with the outcome of spurring innovation specifically in mind. Let me show you how the utilization of these attributes can have that result.

- ENERGETIC: After almost all of my seminars, someone from the class approaches me afterward and says, "This is fun and it's real work!" Damn right innovation is real work.

  Innovation involves more than play and fantasy, it

requires focus, practice, effort, and commitment to a process. You'll find innovation to be fun, active, fulfilling, exciting, and also hard work. Innovation is demanding, it's mentally challenging, it can be exhausting – like anything else worth achieving. Experiencing results from innovation requires energy because those results will only be accomplished through work.

- ENERGIZES OTHER PEOPLE: Communicating to team members the tremendous individual growth and engagement possible through innovation creates tremendous enthusiasm and commitment. An ability to share your passion for innovation and generate excitement around its implementation will motivate employees to contribute their best effort.

- HAS AN EDGE: Having an edge to Jack Welch means being able to make tough decisions. During the innovation process, there are times when difficult decisions need to be made: team composition, the selection of which projects and problems to pursue, which ideas to focus on, which to leave behind and how aggressively to pursue them, and what resources to devote to an idea. Team leaders have many challenges to face and ideas to sift through, an ability to consider all that information and act decisively in the best interest of the group will be vital to innovation's success.

- EXECUTES: Remember my definition of innovation: "The end result. The point at which people pay you for the products and services you've developed." Results will be experienced only after the project comes to completion and that happens through execution. (A secondary interpretation of "execution" applied to innovation surrounds executing the person with the great idea and stealing it for your own.)

A leader modeling himself after Jack Welch will be a leader prepared to foster innovation. Welch ran a highly successful corporation for two decades, but he's only one man. How about the countless number of CEOs, presidents and owners of other successful companies?

Jim Collins' *Good to Great* remains one of my favorite books on business and life. Collins' extensive research attempts to define what separates the companies that are exceptional market-leaders, from those that are merely good. One factor Collins points to – in fact the first factor – he calls "LEVEL 5 LEADERSHIP."

Good to Great describes this type of leader as someone who, "Builds enduring greatness through a paradoxical blend of personal humility and professional will." In essence, this leader subjugates his own ego for the benefit of the company, organization or team. This mindset obviously incorporates and supports attributes I've discussed previously such as collaboration, partnership building and energizing other people. To me it most closely relates to innovation by definitively blowing up the idea of the effectiveness of a Lone Genius.

You recall the Lone Genius, one preferably brilliant individual attempting to meet all the challenges of innovation alone. I previously debunked the efficacy of this person and the ocean of data Collins uses to support the power of his "Level 5 Leader" provides additional support for how autocratic, imperial individuals who attempt to control all aspects of a company, project or initiative, often for the promotion of their own ends, fail in the long run.

The leaders who consistently generate dynamic results through innovation remember that the team and the goal come first. Their recognition and rewards will come later and be inevitable so long as they continually support and emphasize the communication, commitment, collaboration and follow-through necessary for ideas to become innovations.

Collins conducted extensive research on leadership while writing *Good to Great*; FranklinCovey has undertaken similarly exhaustive research on the subject in order to teach and consult businesses on leadership.

Globally preeminent in leadership training and consulting, Franklin Covey holds a leadership seminar titled, "The Four Imperatives of Great Leaders." Those imperatives are:

INSPIRE TRUST

CLARIFY PURPOSE

ALIGN SYSTEMS

UNLEASH TALENT

As with Jack Welch and Collins' "Level 5 Leader," these traits also perfectly apply to innovation.

- INSPIRE TRUST: Contrast the Barbaric Manager with an innovative culture. The Barbaric Manager prevents innovation from taking hold by eroding trust between himself and team members while an innovative culture supports the contribution of individuals by fostering trust between them and their supervisors. Our ideas are personal; we make ourselves vulnerable when we present them. For innovation to flower people must trust their leaders well enough to continue offering the ideas necessary to feed the process.

- CLARIFY PURPOSE: I see "clarifying purpose" as another phrase for "focus;" I've previously written, innovation works best when its aims are well defined.

- ALIGN SYSTEMS: Imagination, creativity, invention,

prototypes, ideation sessions, project management, marketing, market research – generating results from innovation often demands a complex web of individuals and groups working together, for that matrix to be effective, it has to be coordinated and cohesive.

- UNLEASH TALENT: The people on your team right now have the brains, experience and ideas necessary to overcome whatever obstacles or challenges your business may be facing. You don't need an outside consultant or more powerful computers to innovate when you support and engage your people and unleash their talent.

Different skills, different experts, same effect on innovation. Take Welch, take Franklin Covey, take Collins, take them all, take some of each, add what you like, leave what you don't, move down the buffet line of leadership traits and fix yourself of a plate of the dishes you like best. Whichever you pick – strong communicator, risk taker, energy, unleash talent, or any other combination – you can't go wrong.

The characteristics outlined above are traditional, the standards. What if you have a more forward facing view of leadership, will it still support innovation?

"Fast Company" magazine dedicates itself to uncovering what's next in business. Its website featured a commentary written by Brian Ward, a member of the "Fast Company" blogging community and principal of Affinity Consulting. He outlined "The Five Key Facets of Leadership" and listed them as:

FOCUS
AUTHENTICITY
COURAGE
EMPATHY AND TIMING

I'm sure you're starting to see, like all the others, these characteristics apply directly to innovation.

- FOCUS: There's that word again. Innovation becomes most effective when used to solve real customer issues and not as a desperate catchall attempt to address fuzzy demands like "I need more ideas!" or "We need new products!"

- AUTHENTICITY: Is your passion for innovation authentic or is this just the latest fad you're chasing? If you posses a genuine belief in innovation, your group will line up behind you as it observes your commitment. An artificial belief in innovation will eventually be discovered by team members and undermine the process as employees wait for you to ditch innovation for the next hot business-strategy craze. Authenticity will drive energy into you team and be returned to you as trust.

- COURAGE: Innovation will require your team to think differently, it will ask people to take on different responsibilities, and there will be resistance to that change. The courage to move forward with what you believe despite push-back will see you through any rough patches.

  As innovation takes hold, courage will also be required to pursue the ideas generated. Few circumstances surrounding innovation frustrate me more than a team which comes up with a great idea only to be derailed by a leader lacking the courage to green-light a project or commit to the changes necessary to make it happen and follow it through to completion.

- EMPATHY: A great trait we've yet to uncover. When you can understand your customers, their pain points, needs and values and put yourself in a customer or potential customer's shoes, your ability to effectively innovate solutions for them increases dramatically. Conversely, without an ability to understand your customers or market, how can you properly innovate products and services for them?

- TIMING: Innovation's success requires more than developing fantastically imaginative and groundbreaking products, services or process improvements, it requires knowing whether or not the marketplace is ready for them.

Apple innovated its personal digital assistant, the Newton, eight years before the Palm Pilot was introduced. Apple spent $400 million to develop the Newton and it failed miserably because it was vastly ahead of consumer needs. Palm had a budget of $40 million and cornered the market for PDAs long after the Newton's introduction. You can be too far ahead of your time. Knowing what customers are ready for, and what they're not ready for, will provide greater focus to your efforts.

Perhaps no work however more dramatically shows the intimate links between general business leadership and leadership in innovation than Kevin Eikenberry's *Remarkable Leadership*. Eikenberry believes remarkable leaders (emphasis mine throughout):

LEARN CONTINUALLY
CHAMPION CHANGE
COMMUNICATE POWERFULLY
BUILD RELATIONSHIPS
DEVELOP OTHERS
FOCUS ON CUSTOMERS
INFLUENCE WITH IMPACT
THINK AND ACT INNOVATIVELY
VALUE *COLLABORATION* AND TEAMWORK
SOLVE PROBLEMS AND MAKE DECISIONS

TAKE RESPONSIBILITY AND ARE ACCOUNTABLE
MANAGE PROJECTS AND PROCESSES
SET AND SUPPORT GOALS

Remarkable Leadership is not a book about leadership of innovation, but it sure could be. If I were to sit down and write exactly which principles or qualities are necessary to be a leader of innovation, I couldn't have done better than Eikenberry. *Remarkable Leadership* crystallizes how the leadership skills required in the general business world are shared with those which make an effective leader of innovation.

HELPFUL HINT: "You manage things, you lead people," Grace Murray Hopper.

A difference exists between leadership and management and I'd like to take a moment to explain how that difference applies to innovation.

An individual manager serves as a piece of an overall management structure, a deputy in a more or less uniform process of how things get done within an organization. A leader often works independent of specific instructions or defined responsibilities.

Managers are tasked with their responsibilities, chosen for the position by someone higher up. Leaders regularly take their own initiative to accomplish goals and draw their power and effectiveness through the dynamism of their personality and outside of formal titles.

All employees can not be managers, but all employees can be leaders by demonstrating the behaviors I've detailed.

A manager in innovation owns the process and makes final decisions. This employee keeps innovation ongoing and successful. A manager of innovation needs to be on top of project selection and follow through as well as the assignment of tasks and deadlines. The manager needs to determine which tools are used and how frequently ideation sessions are held. The manager acts as the coach and "go-to" person for questions. Organization, oversight, and reporting are the responsibilities of this employee as well as supporting the values of an innovative culture.

Managing the process of innovation demands time and effort to keep projects focused and on-track.

Must your organization have an innovation manager? Not formally, but there has to be order and a process for idea generation and innovation to follow. Someone must assume the responsibility of managing innovation for it to produce results.

Regardless of the position you hold on your team or within your company, don't underestimate your ability to influence people. By demonstrating any of the behaviors I've detailed you are capable of becoming a leader of innovation.

But to lead you have to act. Leadership is philosophy, actually leading demands action, and innovation requires action to deliver results.

If you have a desire to transform yourself, your team, or your company without willingness to take action and help lead the way, you're just complaining. The world bursts at the seams with complainers and daydreamers who refuse to put any action behind their ideas; make your mark by taking the next step and acting.

Innovation can take you and your team to places you've only dreamed about, but it can't work alone, it needs someone to lead the way. Lead the way.

CHAPTER 11
Now Go Do It

When you began reading "Saving Innovation," you had numerous questions about the subject and I hope I've answered most of them.

Now I have a question for you: What are you going to do tomorrow? How are you going to take the lessons of this book and start putting them into practice on your team or at your business tomorrow?

Delaying your attempts to think and act innovatively only extends the length of time it will take you to reach your goals and achieve your dreams. I don't want you to merely understand the concepts I've presented here, for me to succeed in my mission for writing this book, you need to use them. Which ideas you use and how you use them will be individual to your personality, group and challenge.

Think of all the ground we've covered:

- Determining a common language of innovation with specific definitions for commonly used and misused words
- Uncovering why an innovative culture must come before the introduction of tools and understanding how to build that culture

- Instruction on the basic tools necessary to achieve your idea generation goal
- Detailing what it takes to become a leader of innovation

In each of those instances, I gave you a place to start because I wanted to be sure you had something concrete to begin working on tomorrow. That may be as simple as a focus on demonstrating characteristics of a leader of innovation or as involved as planning an off-site observation exercise to spur brainstorming.

Wherever you are in your innovation journey, though, you now have a starting point of your choosing. You know how to take the first step toward fulfilling the promise of innovation; take it, practice that step, celebrate your success and when you and your team feel ready to advance, return to "Saving Innovation" for the next step.

Whichever action you choose becomes the correct one because you are starting. Don't concern yourself with becoming a master of innovation next week or bringing a revolutionary product to market before the end of the fiscal year, that's not realistic. Take one manageable, practical, modest step tomorrow toward improving your innovation efforts and stick with it. Consistency and commitment to that action over time will allow you eventually to achieve your fantastic long-range goals.

If you find your head swimming at the amount of information presented and you're still unsure about where to start, go back to the basics:

1. Understand the language of innovation and get your people talking about innovation properly by sharing it with them. (Chapter 2)

Once they are talking,

2. Examine your team's culture and make sure communication,

candor, curiosity and commitment are being practiced and rewarded. (Chapter 4)

Then,

3. Identify your idea generation goal, develop a focused problem statement, select the appropriate tool and hold a brainstorming session. (Chapter 5, 6, 7, 8)

Throughout,

4. Become a leader of innovation by thinking about how the leadership skills you already posses apply to innovation. (Chapter 9)

Ten thousand dollars worth of innovation consulting in four simple sentences and yes it is that simple. But you have to do it. You have to start, you have to practice, you have to commit and you have to follow through.

I still use and promote those same fundamental steps with my most advanced innovation clients. These are the essential procedures, the essential skills, the "must-have" understandings when it comes to innovation and they will never go out of fashion or lose their effectiveness. I do and you should refer back to them time and again for practice sharpening the elemental skills necessary to experience results from innovation.

I continue to use focused problem statements, brain-writing, observation, and curiosity even with groups I've worked with for years and I always will. Build a solid foundation upon which innovation can grow, repeatedly practice the basics, and prepare for dynamic results.

The ideas in "Saving Innovation" aren't theory or mere speculation; I've seen them work repeatedly with all different people, teams and challenges and I know they'll work for you. I've felt the frustration of managers tasked with becoming more innovative and not knowing where to start. I've heard all the excuses about being too busy and not having enough time to concentrate on innovation.

Instead of accepting those barriers, I synthesized a new approach to innovation focusing on starting points and basics which are applicable to anyone regardless of team, experience or goal. I know that if you make an effort to follow my simple advice regarding the establishment of an innovative culture and the use of basic idea generation tools, your attempts to innovate will progress. Start small, manage expectations, focus on basics and crash through barriers.

As much as you will determine your innovation future, the journey can't be taken alone. I've explained many times the ineffectiveness of the Lone Genius and I want you to be thinking about how to involve as many different people in your group, business or company as possible with the innovation initiatives you are embarking on.

Get help, build a team, build a community, start collaborating and spread your passion for innovation far and wide. Share the strategies of this book, discuss them, encourage coworkers to communicate about innovation and think about how innovation can benefit them and the team. The ideas and techniques detailed in "Saving Innovation" will have greater power to generate results as more people become aware of them.

Innovation isn't exclusive. Wonderfully creative artists don't own it, nor does the new product development team, your research and development division or only the people who've purchased this book. Innovation belongs to everyone. It works for everyone on all challenges and each employee has a unique role they can play in the process which best utilizes their individual talents.

Harness that collective power.

You know what to do. You know how to do it. Now commit. What are you going to do tomorrow?

Make a promise to yourself, your co-workers, your family, and your future, whatever motivates you to drive toward your full potential and goals, resolve yourself to that inspiration and follow through on this pledge.

You now have the ability to harness the incredible power of innovation. Use that power. Use my process of innovation not merely as a limited tool to answer individual business challenges, use my process of innovation as a wide-ranging approach to problem solving.

Innovation's potential – its promise – holds results far greater than bringing new products to market. Innovation's true power – and yours – will be realized when you start viewing my fundamentals of innovation as a way of doing business which animates employee communication and engagement, stimulates imagination and creativity, and opens the minds within an organization to possibilities never thought of before.

Regardless of the specificity of your individual objective – safety, costs, employees, products, customers, productivity, waste – installing the tenets of my process of innovation will help you reach it. Innovation has that power.

If you want to:

- Engage with your customers in ways you've never thought of before. Innovation does.
- Distinguish your brand in a crowded marketplace. Innovation does.

- Develop business in untapped markets. Innovation does.
- Improve diversity. Innovation does.
- Cut costs. Innovation does.
- Energize and empower employees to higher performance. Innovation does.

Innovation promised to solve these problems. That was the potential which excited people. Then businesses and individuals tried applying the innovative practices they were taught. Wanting to use these techniques and not knowing where to get started or how to apply them led only to frustration, not innovation.

You know how to get started and you now posses a detailed, step-by-step process of innovation which is easily applicable and proven to generate results across a complete spectrum of businesses, people, challenges and geographies.

That's exciting. You are in ownership of a not-so-secret weapon developed and proven to overcome all of your business challenges and I'm on the edge of my seat anticipating the future you will create by using it.

About the Authors

MICHAEL DUGAN has created and coached innovation tools, techniques and processes to businesses of all sizes, globally, for more than 10 years. His corporate innovation workshops have resulted in numerous new products, significant sales jumps, improved efficiencies, and inspired employees. He lives in Minneapolis, Minnesota but is more often found in an airplane or airport traveling to work with teams around the world.

CHADD SCOTT is a writer and radio personality living in Atlanta, Georgia.

To contact the authors:
Email: savinginnovation@gmail.com
Twitter: @saveinnovation
Facebook: Saving Innovation

CPSIA information can be obtained
at www.ICGtesting.com
Printed in the USA
FFHW021818150319
51104511-56530FF